TRAVELER'S GUIDE
TO THE ANCIENT WORLD

ANCIENT EGYPT

Metro Books
122 Fifth Avenue
New York, NY 10011

ISBN-13: 978-1-4351-0186-9
ISBN-10: 1-4351-0186-3

Printed and bound in China

1 3 5 7 9 10 8 6 4 2

TRAVELER'S GUIDE
TO THE ANCIENT WORLD

ANCIENT EGYPT

THEBES
AND THE NILE VALLEY

Charlotte Booth

METRO BOOKS
NEW YORK

CONTENTS

SURROUNDING AREAS

ENTERTAINMENT ON A BUDGET

PRACTICAL CONSIDERATIONS

REFERENCES AND RESOURCES

INTRODUCTION: WHEN THIS BOOK WAS WRITTEN

WRITTEN TO OFFER ADVICE TO TRAVELERS TO THE GREAT NATION OF EGYPT AND IN PARTICULAR THE CITY OF THEBES, THIS BOOK IS SET IN 1200 BCE.

A HISTORICAL TIMELINE

Over 2000 years ago	Gods ruled the Earth
1950 years ago	Unification of Egypt for the first time under Narmer
1468 years ago	The Step Pyramid of Djoser is built
1389 years ago	The Great Pyramid of Khufu is built
1078 years ago	Pepy Neferkara ruled for nearly 100 years
940–700 years ago	Egypt is divided
642 years ago	Amenemhat Nymaatra built his pyramid complex at Hawara
550–370 years ago	Egypt is divided
370 years ago	The reign of Ahmose Nebpehtyre and the expulsion of the Heqa Haswt
300 years ago	The reign of Thutmosis Menkheperre the great empire builder
290 years ago	The legendary expedition to Punt in the reign of Thutmosis Menkheperre
280 years ago	The battle of Megiddo won by Thutmosis Menkheperre
186 years ago	The reign of Amenhotep Nebmaatra
120 years ago	Horemheb chose the first king of the Ramesside dynasty
70 years ago	The Founding of Pr-Rameses by Sety Menmaatra
60 years ago	The battle of Kadesh

WHAT TO EXPECT

A HISTORY OF DIVISION

Although Egypt is a largely homogeneous society its landscape is one of extremes, and its political structure is very clearly defined. The Nile runs down the center of Egypt and has determined the history of the country; this great river has created divisions that persist today. The Nile is the life force of the country, with every person and animal relying on it for food, water, pleasure and transportation.

On either side of the Nile is the Nile Valley, which is a fertile strip of land on which everyone in Egypt is settled. To the east and west of the Nile Valley is the unrelenting desert inhabited only by wild animals and Bedouin tribes, separated from the Nile Valley on the west by tall cliffs of rock. However, this is not wasted by the Egyptians: it is the setting for chariot racing and hunts, both for the king and the elite.

The land of Egypt is also divided politically between north and south: the major city is Mennefer in the north, and Thebes (Waset) in the south. Mennefer is the administrative center at this time of writing and Thebes the religious one. Both are cosmopolitan cities with a royal palace. However, there are very distinctive cultural differences between the north and south, with the north inhabited by a large number of Asiatics, especially in the Delta region.

31 years ago	The completion of Abu Simbel by Ramses Usermaatra-Setepenra
Present Day	Year 65 of the reign of Ramses Usermaatra-Setepenra

* Note for the modern reader: For a note on the reliability of these dates see p. 156.

INTRODUCTION: EGYPT AND THE KNOWN WORLD

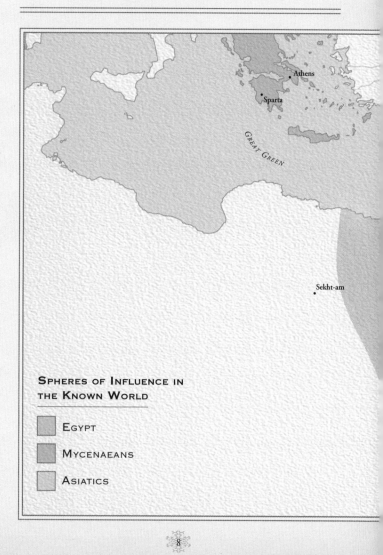

Athens

Sparta

GREAT GREEN

Sekht-am

SPHERES OF INFLUENCE IN
THE KNOWN WORLD

EGYPT

MYCENAEANS

ASIATICS

SITUATED IN NORTH AFRICA, EGYPT IS THE GREATEST OF THE WORLD'S CIVILIZATIONS. IT CONSISTS OF UPPER AND LOWER EGYPT, AS WELL AS NUBIA, AND IT IS BOUNDED BY THE LANDS OF THE ASIATICS, AND THE GREAT GREEN SEA.

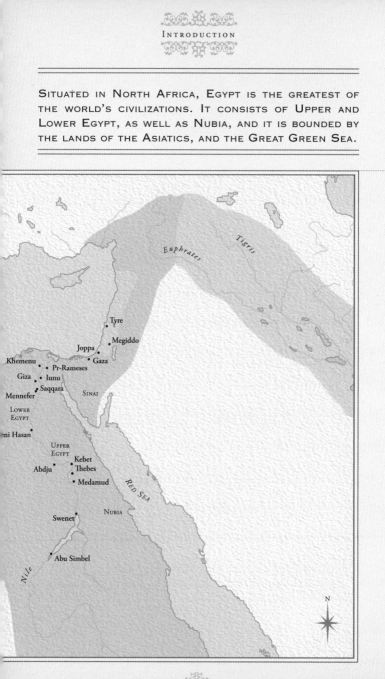

INTRODUCTION: MAKING THE MOST OF YOUR TRIP

EGYPT IS A FANTASTIC PLACE TO VISIT, WITH SOMETHING TO INTEREST EVERYONE. THERE ARE NUMEROUS PLACES OF INTEREST THROUGHOUT THE COUNTRY, WHICH OFFER GLAMOUR, RELIGION, MARKETPLACES, AND GOOD FOOD. THE RELIGIOUS CAPITAL THEBES IN THE SOUTH, HOWEVER, HAS IT ALL, SO IT IS HERE THAT THIS GUIDE WILL FOCUS.

The focus of this guide is Thebes on the east bank of the Nile—the religious capital of Egypt.

Although the king, Ramses, does not live here, it is an important, cosmopolitan city, the site of the royal cemetery and the royal mortuary temples, and is therefore an important spiritual site.

This focus of the region as a royal cemetery ensures that there is a constant supply of wealth in the form of offerings, booty, and taxes to the temples here which are then pumped back into society.

Although Ramses has finished most of his major building works, Thebes is still a hive of activity, with additions and improvements to Ramses' numerous monuments in the area taking place.

There are many things to do in Thebes, such as visiting temples, tombs, markets, participating in hunting and fishing activities, as well as excursions into the desert; but the city of Thebes is also a great starting point for trips into Nubia in the south, and also sites further north such as Abydos.

LANGUAGE AND DIALECTS

The language is very different between the north and the south of Egypt with distinct dialects for most large cities—so much so that there is a well-known local saying: "They are like the words of a man of the Delta when he converses with a man of Elephantine." This dialect issue will obviously be problematic for the tourist, but if simple phrases are spoken slowly and clearly this should be sufficient to make yourself understood.

THE FLOODS OF THE NILE

Needless to say, as a desert environment Egypt is going to be very hot, and therefore this has to be taken into account when planning your trip.

There is also the added complication of the Nile inundation, which leaves most of the country under water for four months in the summer of every year. It is just as well that during these months the weather is unbearably hot and most travelers want to avoid the country at this time. However, that aside, the inundation is a rather magical and picturesque time when even the temples are flooded; so you may see just the tops of pillars or pylons emerging from the swirling waters.

However, with the water and the heat come the mosquitoes, some of which carry unpleasant diseases—so it is important to take these things into account. If you want to see the flood at its height, you should take a trip to the south in midsummer, or to the north a little bit later. By the end of the fourth summer month, the waters will have abated and the farmers be tending the fields.

WHEN TO VISIT

The ideal time for a visit to Egypt is the winter months, when the weather is warm during the day and cool in the evening. Bear in mind when planning your trip that the north of Egypt, although cooler than the south, is very humid and in the summer months can be quite unbearable; and in the winter it can rain.

If you visit when it is hot, it is essential to drink lots of fluid to prevent dehydration. The most common drink is beer; this is available in varying strengths and can be quite refreshing. It is also essential to protect your skin and head from the relentless sunshine. Keep your head covered with either a linen headdress or a wig, as the Egyptians do, and ensure you moisturize your skin with oil or unguents. It is best to cover the skin when in the sun to prevent burns, and there is nothing better for this than the Egyptian linen tunics.

A CONCISE
BACKGROUND

The history of Egypt is a long and varied one.
Over the course of 2,000 years many changes
and developments have led to the great society that
Egypt is today; a country that prospers under the rule
of the god-king Ramses Usermaatra-Setepenra.

HISTORY: GODS TO PHAROAHS

IN THE TIME BEFORE KING NARMER (SOME 2,000 YEARS AGO), THE GODS RULED EGYPT. THE GREATEST OF THESE GODS WAS OSIRIS. HE WAS A BENEVOLENT AND WISE KING, AND THE PERIOD HE RULED IS CONSIDERED A GOLDEN AGE. HE TAUGHT THE EGYPTIAN PEOPLE HOW TO LIVE, HOW TO WORSHIP THE GODS, HOW TO OBEY LAWS, AND EVEN HOW TO IRRIGATE THE LAND—MAKING THEM INDEPENDENT FROM THE DEITIES. ALL KINGS SINCE THAT TIME HAVE EMULATED THIS GREAT GOD AND ARE OFTEN DEPICTED DIGGING IRRIGATION CANALS IN THE MANNER OF OSIRIS (INSET).

It is essential that all kings can prove that their family tree can be traced to these gods, and if they are unable to show this connection then they are not considered to be true kings of Egypt. There were ten divine rulers before the mortal kings gained control:

The first god was Ptah, the creator god, who created all things simply by speaking their names.

Ra (Atum), was the first god created by Ptah, and is the god of the first sunrise.

Shu, the god of the air and the oldest son of Ra (Atum).

Geb was the son of Shu and the god of the earth.

Osiris was Geb's oldest son, and he went on to become the god of the underworld following his brutal murder at the hands of his brother Seth.

Seth is the god of chaos, and also Osiris' brother. He murdered Osiris, and some see him as a usurper.

Horus is the son of Osiris and his rightful heir. The king of Egypt is always associated with him.

Thoth is the god of writing and knowledge, he is also considered as an arbitrator, a position that befits his wisdom.

After the rule of Thoth came Horus, in his second incarnation. He was followed by *Akh spirits*—the blessed dead—those who have been reborn into the afterlife.

Then began the reign of mortals, who are the ancient ancestors of the current king Ramses.

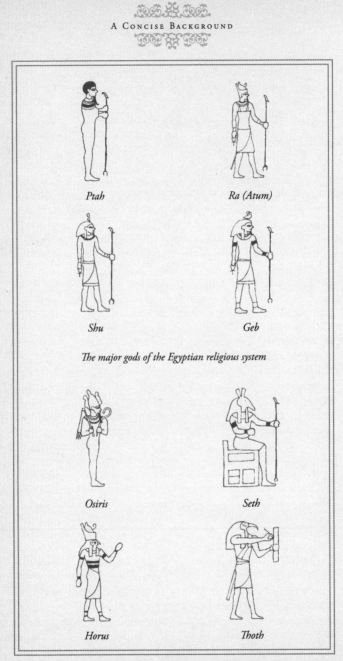

Ptah

Ra (Atum)

Shu

Geb

The major gods of the Egyptian religious system

Osiris

Seth

Horus

Thoth

HISTORY: FROM NARMER TO THE PYRAMIDS

BEFORE THE UNIFICATION OF EGYPT UNDER NARMER, EGYPT WAS DIVIDED INTO NUMEROUS AREAS RULED BY PETTY RULERS. THEN NARMER BECAME THE SOLE KING, AND ALL THE PETTY RULERS ANSWERED TO HIM, ALTHOUGH THEY STILL HAD SOME CONTROL OVER THEIR LOCAL REGIONS. THE STATE WAS GRADUALLY FORMED INTO THE SYSTEM OF GOVERNMENT THAT IS STILL USED IN EGYPT TODAY.

One of the most important developments of this period was the use of hieroglyphic writing. Although invented by the god Thoth, in the time when the gods ruled Egypt, it was only during the reign of Narmer that it was first used by mortals. Initially used for labeling boxes and jars, then for sealing correspondence, boxes, and doors, it was only in the "Pyramid Age" that hieroglyphic writing became more widely used.

By the end of this period the state was fully formed, and the king, gaining in power, was able to afford elaborate funerary monuments and grave goods.

THE OLD KINGDOM

The Pyramid Age, around 1,400 years ago, was an economically sound and politically stable period, characterized by the construction of large funerary monuments. However, it was a slow series of advancements that led from the *mastaba* (bench-like) tombs of the earliest kings to the greatest pyramids. The design of the mastaba was extended by King Djoser, to build the first pyramid at Saqqara, and this stepped design was further improved over the course of the next hundred years until a "true" pyramid was created.

The greatest pyramid builder was Sneferu, who built two pyramids at Dashur. The first was beset by problems, caused by a miscalculation of the required angle of the slope given the weight of the stones used, but the second was perfect. The next king, Khufu, simply took this design and enlarged it in order to build his monument at Giza.

Although the economy of the Pyramid Age was strong, there were periods of instability, even during the reign of Djoser, due to bad harvests and famine. Djoser was advised by his vizier to appeal to the god Khnum, who resides at the source of the Nile, and the economy subsequently improved.

However, towards the end of the Pyramid Age, in the reign of Tety, the economy began to crumble, when the king began granting tax exemptions to maintain the loyalty of his courtiers. This mistake, which Egyptians hope will never be repeated, meant that the nobles became wealthier than the king, so the royal pyramids became smaller and the noble tombs larger and more elaborate; although both are well worth visiting if you get the chance.

THE GREAT ANCESTOR

The most important king of this early period, some 2,000 years ago, was Narmer (depicted on the "palette of Narmer"). He ruled at a time when Egypt was divided among many kingdoms. Narmer was the first to rule under the law of Maat, and by uniting these petty chieftains he ensured Egypt was ruled by one king. This unification, the first large-scale unification of a civilization, was the culmination of lots of small campaigns pushing north from his residence in the south, until he had conquered the Asiatic tribes in the north and the Delta. Narmer was also the first king to be aided by the god Horus in his campaigns, underlining his divine right to rule.

HISTORY: THE MIDDLE AND NEW KINGDOMS

AT THE END OF THE PYRAMID AGE, EGYPT WAS WEAK AND DIVIDED, WITH NUMEROUS RULERS GOVERNING SMALL AREAS. IT WASN'T UNTIL THE REIGN OF MENTUHOTEP NEBHETEPRE, SOME 1,200 YEARS AGO, THAT EGYPT WAS REUNITED— ALTHOUGH THE POWER OF THE KING STILL RELIED ON THESE LOCAL RULERS. BY THE END OF SENUSRET KHAKHAURE'S REIGN, 200 YEARS LATER, THE KING WAS POWERFUL ENOUGH NOT TO BE RELIANT ON THESE LOCAL GOVERNORS.

Although what is now considered as the Pyramid Age was finished, the kings of the Middle Kingdom still built pyramids to be buried in, and one of the most impressive is that of Amenemhat Nymaatra at Hawara, which is well worth a visit. Despite the political problems of the period, the boundaries of Egypt continued to be expanded.

The later king Amenemhat Sehetepre fortified the northern borders of the eastern Delta against the Asiatic threat; while Senusret Kheperkara and Senusret Khakhaure extended the southern boundaries of Egypt into Nubia building 17 fortresses to underline Egypt's might, control access to the gold mines and stone quarries, and keep the Nubians in check.

THE NEW KINGDOM

This laid the groundwork for the empire-building of the common era. However, meanwhile Egypt was once again divided, with the Heqa Haswt ruling in the north and eventually all Egypt. It was only the military prowess of the family of Ahmose Nebpehtyre that led to their expulsion; after which it took some time for Egypt to become the strong nation that it is today.

The first great king of this New Kingdom was Thutmosis Menkheperre, who built much of

The Bent Pyramid of Sneferu.

JEWELRY MAKERS

The period of the Middle Kingdom saw the finest jewelry made from beads and gold—it is well worth buying some as a souvenir.

Despite creating beautiful objects, jewelry makers are far from revered. In the *Satire of the Trades*, written during the Middle Kingdom, a jewelry maker is described as having fingers "like a crocodile's" and stinking "more than fish roe," hardly an endearing description! However, each is highly skilled in one aspect of the production process. Metalworkers melt and cast gold, silver, and copper; bead-makers use bow drills to hollow semi-precious stones before polishing the finished bead; while others string these beads onto flax thread to create the final piece.

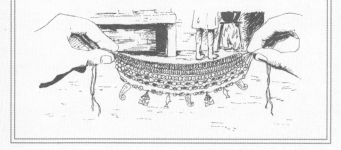

the empire, spending most of his adult life on campaign, capturing hundreds of cities for Egypt.

A founding stone of this new era was the introduction of a standing army. Prior to this time, armies were raised as the need arose, but now the permanent army provides the opportunity for men to seek military careers—and the resulting discipline has made Egypt's forces formidable. A number of great kings of our own era have arisen through the ranks, including the father of Thutmosis Menkheperre, Thutmosis Akheperkara, the great Horemheb; and the father of the current king Ramses, Sety Menmaatra.

The common era has been one of innovations, with the introduction of the wheel, used for chariots, siege warfare, and day-to-day transportation; bellows for metalworking; and the discovery of bronze, allowing stronger and sharper weapons. Another invention, the composite bow, has improved Egypt's military dominance over her enemies, allowing archers to attain more accuracy at greater distances.

POLITICS: THE RULE OF KINGS

EGYPT'S HISTORY IS FILLED WITH HUNDREDS OF KINGS. ALL KINGS ARE DIVINE, INCARNATIONS OF THE GOD HORUS, AND EACH RULES BOTH UPPER AND LOWER EGYPT (SEE P. 22) UNDER THE LAW OF MAAT, AIMING TO EXPAND THE EMPIRE AND PROTECT ITS BORDERS. HOWEVER, ALTHOUGH ALL ARE DIVINE, A FEW HAVE STOOD OUT.

KHUFU

An early king, Khufu ruled for 24 years, around 1,300 years ago. The builder of the largest pyramid at Giza, he was the son of the great Sneferu and Queen Hetepheres. He had at least four wives, and a number of children including the kings Djedefra and Khafra.

His greatest legacy is the Great Pyramid, which took 20 years to build and is the biggest structure in the known world. His master-builder was his cousin Hemon, who is buried in a nearby cemetery.

Despite his legacy, Khufu had a reputation as a tyrant. In the *Tales of Wonder*, written 500 years later, Khufu is represented as spoilt and lecherous, demanding that he be entertained by 20 semi-naked young women rowing him on the pleasure lake of his palace. Another "rumor" concerns the middle satellite pyramid, possibly that of his daughter, who he apparently put to work in a brothel in order to be able to pay for it. However, whether this is true or not, we shall never know.

The Great Pyramid at Giza, the legacy of King Khufu.

THUTMOSIS MENKHEPERRE

Approximately 300 years ago, Thutmosis ruled Egypt for 54 years. He came to the throne as a young boy after the death of his father. Thutmosis spent his youth training with the army; then, in year 23 of his reign, he started campaigning in the Near East to re-establish lost territory. This saw his great victory at Megiddo, which was held by the Hittites. Instead of entering the town by the easy route, Thutmosis showed his courage and ingenuity by taking a difficult path, that only allowed the soldiers to enter in single file, taking the lead himself.

In less than five months Thutmosis had captured three Syrian cities, including Megiddo and Joppa, and returned to Thebes in victory. Over the next 18 years of his reign he traveled to Syria annually, capturing another 350 cities and expanding Egypt's borders further than they had ever been before.

AMENHOTEP NEBMAATRA

Amenhotep was the last great king before the family of the current king took over the throne. The son of Thutmosis Menkheperre and the Great Royal Wife Mutemwia, Amenhotep achieved much during his 38-year rule.

His chief wife was Tiye, although he is rumored to have had over a thousand women in his harem. He was also considered a great hunter, and he issued two commemorative scarabs recording a lion hunt during which he killed 102 lions.

Although he did not fight many battles, Amenhotep improved the economy of Egypt tenfold through extensive mining of gold in the Wadi Hammamat and Kush as well as by increasing trade with the Asiatic territories. This wealth was used to fund a number of building projects, including the mortuary temple on the west bank at Thebes, and vast improvements to the temple of Luxor, which, even after the work of the current king, is still regarded as Amenhotep's temple.

A record of Amenhotep's famous bull hunt.

POLITICS: THE GOVERNANCE OF EGYPT

THE EARLIEST SYSTEM OF GOVERNANCE WAS THE DIVISION OF EGYPT INTO 42 NOMES (BOROUGHS): 22 IN THE NORTH AND 20 IN THE SOUTH. ALTHOUGH ALL ARE ANSWERABLE TO THE KING, EACH NOME HAS A NOMARCH OR MAYOR, WHO GOVERNS THE LOCAL AREA AND REPORTS BACK TO THE VIZIER, WHO INFORMS THE KING.

Each nome also has its own capital city, local deity, and temple, as well as religious taboos and rituals. Each nome is asked to make an annual tribute of local resources to the king, and is identifiable by a local standard, bearing the statue of a local deity, animal, or plant.

The most important ideological division of Egypt is into north and south. South Egypt is known as Upper Egypt, and Lower Egypt is the north; collectively they are referred to as the "Two Lands." It is essential for all true kings, following the rule of Narmer, to rule over a united Egypt, and only a true king holds the title "King of Upper and Lower Egypt."

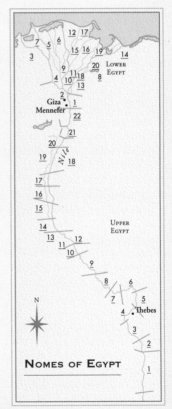

NOMES OF EGYPT

The numbered nomes (administrative boroughs) of Egypt.

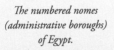

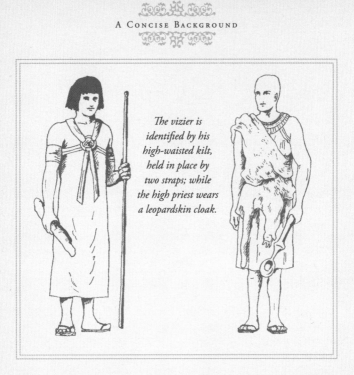

The vizier is identified by his high-waisted kilt, held in place by two straps; while the high priest wears a leopardskin cloak.

EAST AND WEST

Egypt can also be divided along the east and west banks of the Nile. The west bank is mostly used for cemeteries and mortuary temples, as it in the west that the sun sets. In fact, the deceased are said to "reside in the west." The east bank, on the other hand, is the "land of the living" and this is where you will find the villages and cult temples. However, there are always exceptions to the rule, so you shouldn't be surprised if you happen to see a village on the west bank or even a cemetery on the east.

THE HIGHEST OFFICE

Egyptian society is organized with the king at the top, and the importance of officials is related to their proximity to him. Power is centered around three positions, and should they ever come to be held by one man, his power would arguably be greater than the king's.

The most important of the three is the vizier, a close advisor to the king, who controls the running of the palace and state; after him, power is held by a military general and the High Priest of Amun, who protect the physical and spiritual wellbeing of the population.

POLITICS: THE STRUCTURE OF SOCIETY

AN INDIVIDUAL'S POSITION WITHIN EGYPTIAN SOCIETY IS CLOSELY ASSOCIATED WITH THEIR OCCUPATION. THE STRUCTURE OF THAT SOCIETY REFLECTS THE RELATIVE ABUNDANCE OF SKILLS; FOR EXAMPLE, THE MULTITUDINOUS SERVANTS AND FARMERS FORM THE LOWER CLASSES, WHILE THE RARIFIED SKILLS OF THE PRIESTS, SCHOLARS AND SCRIBES ENSURE THAT THEY OCCUPY THE UPPER ECHELONS OF SOCIETY.

TEMPLE PRIESTS

The majority of the temple priesthood are part-time, working for one month in every four (three months a year). They do not have access to the sacred statue, but rather carry out the more mundane tasks that are necessary in the running of a busy temple. Only a handful of priests are employed on a full-time basis.

SCRIBES AND SCHOLARS

Literacy levels are high in Egypt compared to much of the known world, but scribes and scholars are still revered, as only around one in a hundred people can read. Most villages have a scribe for local needs, while others work in temple, military, or palace administration. The most revered scholars are the lector priests, as they have access to the ancient and sacred texts, and the great secrets that they hold.

CRAFTSMEN

A little further down the social scale from scribes are craftsmen, such as those living at the "Place of Truth" responsible for creating the royal tombs in the Valleys of the Kings and Queens. These artists, stonemasons, and carpenters are at the top of their profession, and are well paid, and well respected.

FARMERS

Farmers are particularly important in the Egyptian economy, being responsible for the production of all Egypt's food. The majority of farmland in Thebes is owned by Karnak temple, and rented to the farmers. They pay tax and rent from their yield, which goes into the temple stores to be redistributed as wages to the craftsmen, priests, palace personnel, and also the military.

SERVANTS

Most elite Egyptians have household servants to aid with day-to-day activities. However, some villages have a central pool of servants for all the villagers at an hourly fee, helping those who can't afford a full-time servant.

Servants range from water-carriers, wet-nurses for newborn children, butlers, cleaners, people to tend to the animals, and even fan-bearers for the royal household.

WHAT TO EXPECT

THE IMPORTANCE OF DRESS

The Egyptians are traditionalists, and like those of certain classes and occupations to dress in a particular way, making them easy to identify. The average Egyptian dresses simply, in either a white linen tunic that reaches the floor—sleeveless in the summer and long-sleeved in the winter—or a short tunic with a white kilt. The quality of linen is also identifiable by its fineness, so transparent linen is a sign of wealth. As well as a person's wealth, it is also possible to identify their occupation from their clothes. For example, a scribe is identifiable by his palette slung over his shoulder, and his ink-stained fingers, while a bald man in a white kilt with a leopardskin cloak is a high priest, and a wigged man in a similar cloak is likely to be a *sem* (funerary) priest. If you spot a man with a long kilt tied under the armpits and held around the neck by two straps, then be careful—you are in the presence of the vizier and therefore the most powerful man in Thebes after the king.

RELIGION: THE GODS OF EGYPT

MANY DEITIES ARE WORSHIPPED IN AND AROUND THEBES, OF WHOM THE MOST IMPORTANT IS AMUN (INSET), THE CREATOR AND SUN GOD WORSHIPPED AT KARNAK AND LUXOR TEMPLES. ON THE WEST BANK OF THE NILE A NUMBER OF OTHER DEITIES ARE WORSHIPPED AT THE TOWN OF DEIR EL MEDINA, INCLUDING THE COBRA GODDESS MERETSEGAR, WHO PROTECTS AGAINST SCORPION AND SNAKE BITES; THE CREATOR GOD PTAH, PATRON OF WORKMEN; AND HATHOR, THE MOTHER GODDESS WHO ALSO REPRESENTS BEAUTY, SEXUAL LOVE, AND FRIVOLITY. WHATEVER YOUR POSITION OR STATUS THERE IS SURE TO BE A THEBAN DEITY TO SUIT YOUR NEEDS.

THE SOLAR CULT AT IUNU

Although the majority of Egyptian temples are dedicated to a sun god or goddess, or at least one with solar connections, the main city for solar worship is in the northern site of Iunu, where the large temple of Ra-Horakhty is situated. The first solar temple was built here some 1,400 years ago and was of such proportions that it could be seen from many of the pyramid fields, including that of Giza, on the opposite side of the Nile. This site has remained a center of solar worship ever since.

Iunu is a fundamental part of the solar beliefs in Egypt, as it is the site where the mound of creation, upon which all life began, erupted from the primeval waters. This belief is mentioned in the Pyramid Texts, and therefore dates back to the earliest history of Egypt. The supreme creator is Atum, who created the next generation of gods from his semen. They in turn created the next generation, and so on until the current king Ramses was conceived.

Although Atum originated at the site, the main god worshipped here today is Ra-Horakhty, who has the body of a human, but the head of a hawk, being a confluence of Ra and Horus. As early as 1,400 years ago the cult at Iunu was so powerful that it greatly influenced the kingship ideology, and many kings have since integrated Ra into their own names, and added the title "Son of Ra" to their title to emphasize their divinity. The influence of the god Ra has since entered the funerary sphere, with many royal tombs in Thebes bearing the "Litany of Ra" on the walls, in which Ra is associated with Osiris, the god of the underworld, and is therefore essential to the rebirth of the king.

Ra-Horakhty, the hawk-headed embodiment of Ra and Horus.

The Vizier of The Humble

Many visitors to Thebes are on pilgrimage to the oracle of the god Amun, who is the main god of the region.

Amun is known as the "vizier of the humble" and is both just and fair. There are two ways of approaching Amun with a request, and no question is considered too small or insignificant. If you are in Thebes during a festival, then you will see the god paraded through the streets in his sacred bark, allowing you to address him directly. If, however, you would like a more discreet communion, or if no processions are planned, then you can approach the temple itself with your request or question written down. The priest, upon payment of a fee, will present this to Amun on your behalf.

RELIGION: LIFE AFTER DEATH

EGYPTIANS BELIEVE THAT THE DECEASED HAVE THE OPPORTUNITY TO BE REBORN IN THE AFTERLIFE PROVIDED THEY FULFILL CERTAIN CRITERIA, SUCH AS MUMMIFICATION, AND A BURIAL COMPLETE WITH CERTAIN RITUALS INCLUDING THE "OPENING OF THE MOUTH," THE "WEIGHING OF THE HEART," AND THE CONSTANT REPETITION OF THEIR NAME BY THE LIVING.

The living play an important role in the afterlife, being responsible for the physical and spiritual sustenance of the dead. Offerings help ensure an eternity in the Amduat—believed to be much like Egypt at its best, with a river bisecting it, abundant vegetation, animals, and fish.

MUMMIFICATION

The dead are preserved before burial through the process of mummification, to ensure a functioning body for the afterlife. The whole process takes 70 days, and is carried out by embalmers who work from temporary structures in the cemeteries on the west bank. The first 35 days or so are concerned with drying out the body, starting with the removal of the internal organs. The brain is removed through a nostril using a long copper hook, and the internal organs are removed through a slit in the left-hand side of the abdomen. The only organ left in place is the heart, as it is the center of all thought, emotion, and intelligence. The cavities left are washed with palm wine and packed with natron.

Once prepared, the body is laid out, completely covered with natron, and left to dry. When the body is dry the natron is removed and its cavities are packed with sawdust, linen, and spices, before being wrapped in linen. This process is overseen by a priest who recites prayers and incantations as each limb is wrapped. Amidst the wrappings numerous amulets are placed in order to protect the deceased in the afterlife.

A sem priest carries out the Opening of the Mouth.

WHAT TO EXPECT

THE EMBALMER'S APPRENTICE

If you visit the west bank, don't be surprised to see a young lad being chased through the streets, with his superiors, and even passers-by, shouting abuse and throwing rocks. Don't call the Medjay (see p. 37)—this is just a ritual. The embalmer's apprentice, who makes the first cut into the torso, needs to be punished for this violation; hence the spectacle in the street. Feel free to join in and add your own abuses to the chorus—it is all part of his job, after all!

WEIGHING THE HEART

A key part of Egyptian funerary beliefs is that before the deceased are reborn in the afterlife they enter the Hall of Judgment—presided over by Osiris, god of the underworld. Here their heart is weighed against the goddess Maat, who represents truth and balance. If the heart weighs more than Maat it will be devoured by a demon, leaving the deceased in limbo. The ideal situation is where the heart and Maat weigh the same.

In order to ensure this, the deceased recites the "Negative Confession," a list of wrongs they haven't committed. A heart scarab, which is encouraged not to betray these wrongs, is placed within the mummy wrappings.

THE BOOK OF THE DEAD

Funerary texts act as guidebooks, giving information for the journey into the afterlife, including names of doors and locks, and incantations to repel harm. There are also images of the dead meeting protective demons and gatekeepers.

The *Book of the Dead* is the most popular of these texts, derived from the "Coffin Texts" of 500 or so years ago, which themselves derived from the much older "Pyramid Texts."

The Weighing of the Heart.

DOMESTIC LIFE: FAMILY AND THE ROLE OF WOMEN

HOME LIFE IS VERY IMPORTANT TO THE EGYPTIANS, AND THE EXTENDED FAMILY IS A MAJOR PART OF THIS. SOMETIMES AS MANY AS 15 PEOPLE MAY LIVE IN THE SAME TWO-STORY MUD-BRICK HOUSE, WITH UP TO THREE GENERATIONS UNDER ONE ROOF. MARRIAGE TAKES PLACE AT AN EARLY AGE, GENERALLY WITHIN RATHER THAN BETWEEN SOCIAL CLASSES, BUT AS A GENERAL RULE IT IS NOT ARRANGED BY THE FAMILIES.

Most girls marry as soon as they are of child-bearing age, generally between 12 and 15 years old. On the other hand, some men choose to concentrate on their careers first, building up wealth and status before starting a family. It is not unusual to see girls of 12 married to men of 30 or even older.

There is no elaborate ceremony, and the act of getting married is simply that the bride moves into the home of her new husband. Local villages may have a procession through the streets to mark the occasion, as a means of showing off the bride's dowry. This dowry remains the property of the woman and she can do with it as she wants: sell it, bequeath it, or simply keep it. Marriage contracts are only drawn up if the couple are particularly wealthy, and often provide for the division of property should they divorce.

On the streets of Thebes you may be surprised to hear married couples refer to each other as "brother" and "sister," but these are simply terms of endearment and do not refer to any blood relationship. It is a social taboo for siblings to marry, unless they are in the royal family, although marriage between cousins or half-siblings is considered acceptable, albeit uncommon. It is also unacceptable for a man to have more than one wife, but he may have concubines.

The simplicity of getting married is reflected by the process of divorce, in which either the husband or the wife simply declares "I divorce you." The wife then takes her possessions back to her family home, including her dowry, and, if the man was at fault, a third of his property as well. It is perfectly acceptable for either partner to remarry should they wish.

Families in Egypt are large and it is not unusual for a couple to have up to ten children. Infant mortality rates are high and few children survive beyond five. It is considered essential for families to have at least one surviving son, to take over the occupation of his father upon his death, as well as to take care of his parents in old age. Although girls are more expensive, as they take a dowry, female infanticide is not practiced as all children are considered sacred—though boys are preferred to girls.

THE ROLE OF WOMEN

Egyptian women are equal to men of the same class in most instances, and it is common to see unaccompanied women haggling at the harbor, or peddling their own products on the riverbank. There are no restrictions on men and women doing business with each other, even if they are unrelated, and women often earn a separate income from their husbands.

Women can do anything a man can, including buying, selling, inheriting, or bequeathing property; they can sue anyone of the same class; and can bear witness to legal documents, provided of course that they are literate.

Although most women are not educated, this is not because it is not permitted, but rather a question of whether a family can afford an education for its daughters as well as its sons. However, a popular

Egyptian women share many of the rights of men. In fact you can meet many of them buying and selling goods by the riverbank.

saying is that "Teaching a woman is like having a sack of grain with the side split," as more often than not they will marry and not use their education.

Even if educated to a high standard, women are unable to work in official administration alongside men. In the 2,000 years of Egyptian history to date, there have been only a handful of female scribes, or overseers, the main restriction being that they are unable to control the work of men. Therefore women tend to work in households (their own or those of the rich), as the head of staff, or housekeeper, or in those industries that are dominated by women, such as dressmaking, wigmaking, or even as female physicians.

DOMESTIC LIFE: EDUCATION AND CAREERS

AN EDUCATION IS AVAILABLE TO ALL WHO CAN AFFORD IT, MALE OR FEMALE, ALTHOUGH IT IS MOSTLY BOYS WHO ARE EDUCATED. THERE ARE NO ORGANIZED LEARNING INSTITUTIONS WITHIN THE WIDER COMMUNITY, AND CHILDREN LEARN WHEREVER A SCRIBE SETS UP A TEACHING GROUP. HOWEVER, THERE ARE OFFICIAL CENTERS OF LEARNING FOR THE ELITE.

Many temples accommodate what is known as "The House of Life," an institution managed by the lector priests for teaching priests about the sacred texts and rituals used at the temple. The House of Life also teaches the royal and elite physicians their trade, as well as acting as an archive for hundreds of texts. Royal princes are taught within the palace, and lucky boys of noble families are taught alongside them.

An average education starts with basic writing skills when the child is about five years old. Initially children learn to write in cursive script, then as they progress—if they look likely candidates for a scribal career—they are taught hieroglyphs. Children are taught using the dictation method, in which a scribe reads out a classical text (sometimes as much as a thousand years old), and the children write it down, to be later corrected by the scribe. These texts include model letters, which act as examples of good grammar and vocabulary, as well as "wisdom texts" that provide advice on the correct way to act and live.

By the age of nine a student must decide on a future career—whether military, administrative, or clerical—and will then pass into an apprenticeship before becoming a full employee.

CAREER OPTIONS

For an average Egyptian boy there are a few career options. The eldest son traditionally follows in his father's footsteps, training as an apprentice from a young age and taking over the trade upon his father's death.

Other sons, depending on their skills, may choose a military career—with its promise of travel, good pay, and excitement—or they can enter the priesthood, either in

The writing tools of an Egyptian scribe, one of the better careers available to an Egyptian boy.

a secular position or as part of the ancillary staff. Educated boys with a talent for writing may follow a career either as a local village scribe with a regular income, or even as a member of the royal, military, or temple administration—all well-paid careers with good opportunities for advancement.

Girls, on the other hand, have a more limited choice, as most are expected to marry and stay at home to look after the family. However, some women work in home industries such as linen weaving, baking, and brewing. Some wealthier women make a living by offering loans of silver and copper at hefty interest rates.

MIDWIFERY

With women having up to ten children each from the age of 12 onward, the midwife's role is a crucial one. Some are professionally trained at the temple of Neith at Sais, and are destined for roles within the palace, or among the elite of society.

For the thousands of ordinary women there is a locally trained midwife, who from a young age learns alongside the resident midwife, until she is skilled enough to attend births on her own. Most births are also accompanied by incantations invoking the deities Bes and Taweret to aid the birth and scare off harmful demons. The pregnant woman places a birthing brick, representative of the goddess Meskenet, under each foot, and ivory wands carved with protective imagery touch her person during her labor.

AGRICULTURE AND INDUSTRY

LIKE ANY MAJOR ECONOMY BASED ON A CENTRALIZED STATE, THE IMPORTANCE OF TRADE, FOOD PRODUCTION, AND INDUSTRY IN EGYPT IS PARAMOUNT. ALTHOUGH THESE ELEMENTS ARE OFTEN OVERLOOKED, THE MAJORITY OF EGYPTIANS WORK IN ONE OF THESE FIELDS AND ARE THEREFORE INDIRECTLY RESPONSIBLE FOR THE SMOOTH RUNNING OF THE STATE.

International trade is particularly important to the economy of Egypt, with many items being imported from far and wide. Gold, ebony, ivory, wild animals (including leopards, monkeys, and giraffes), and certain stones, are all imported from Nubia in the south. Lapis lazuli is imported from Afghanistan, albeit via third-party traders. Cedar wood is imported from Byblos, from where ships, sailors, and shipbuilders also arrive. Silver comes from the islands to the north, and although it was once more valuable than gold, it is now cheaper, because of the increased supply. A number of perfumed and vegetable oils are imported from Syria, and are highly valued by Egyptians.

AGRICULTURE

Agriculturists form the majority of the population. Despite their crucial role they perform the worst-paid and the hardest jobs, and as it is considered unskilled work, farmers come from the uneducated echelons of society. In most cases the entire household will help with the harvest. Most

An Egyptian farmer tends his fields.

farmers rent their land from the temple or the palace directly, and pay rent and taxes from their yield. Anything that is left over can be kept. The burden of bad harvests falls particularly heavily on farmers as they work just as hard as normal, only to hand most of the meager yield over to the state. They are also threatened with beatings, should specified quotas not be reached.

INDUSTRY

Egypt is a great producer of many items, some of which are exported to the Near East. Linen is one such valuable export, and is produced in workshops attached to the larger temples, and royal harems, where the close work is carried out by the higher-status queens. Some of the finest artists, stone masons, and carpenters, who work for the king, live in the Place of Truth in Thebes and produce many items of note.

In the capital of Pr-Rameses there are numerous faience factories, producing thousands of decorative colored tiles used in temples and palaces. Further south in the Theban region there are some of the best vineyards, producing wine, which is exported throughout the known world.

WHAT TO EXPECT

LOCAL CROPS

A variety of grains and cereals are grown in Egypt, and although there is a good trade network, most food is produced locally, including barley—used to make beer, the staple drink of adults and children alike—and emmer, einkorn, and spelt, wheats used to make bread. (The grain used is shown by the shape of the loaf.)

Many farmers, and indeed households, grow a variety of produce including small, sweet onions to be eaten raw; garlic for flavoring; peas, lentils, and beans for thickening stews and soups; radishes, cabbages, cucumbers, and lettuces; dates for flavoring beer and to be eaten whole; and a deliciously wide variety of figs.

Many farmers also grow sesame and castor to make oil, as well as flax for the production of linen. They also harvest tree fibers that are used for making baskets and rope.

THE ARMED FORCES

IT WAS ONLY IN THE MODERN ERA THAT THE STANDING ARMY WAS INTRODUCED, AND IN THE LAST 400 YEARS IT HAS BECOME FEARED THROUGHOUT THE KNOWN WORLD. THE ARMY CONSISTS OF NUMEROUS DIVISIONS OF 5,000 MEN EACH (INCLUDING INFANTRY, ARCHERS, SPEARMEN, AND CHARIOTEERS), FURTHER DIVIDED INTO HOSTS OF 500, COMPANIES OF 250, PLATOONS OF 50, AND SQUADS OF 10. THIS MILITARY MACHINE ENSURES THAT EACH SOLDIER CAN BE CAREFULLY GOVERNED, TRAINED, AND CONTROLLED.

The Egyptian military is well armed for any task, with a number of weapons, some traditional and others more recently introduced.

The most basic projectile weapons used are stones, either thrown by hand or with a sling; while throwing sticks, initially used for hunting, are also effective in combat.

Crafted weapons include stone maces for clubbing opponents; bows and arrows, which have a maximum range of just over 550 cubits; spears for throwing or stabbing; and axes, daggers, and swords for close combat.

The Egyptian soldier is lightly armored, wearing a leather over-kilt and carrying a full-body shield approximately three cubits tall made of solid wood, or of a wooden frame covered in hide.

The army is employed in a number of roles besides that of waging war against Egypt's enemies. These include guarding trading routes, transporting stone for sarcophagi and obelisks, and even helping with the harvest. The military is also involved with tax collecting and policing. At present the most heavily policed area is the Valley of the Kings, although this security appears relatively ineffective as many of the tombs have been robbed and desecrated.

There are also numerous ancillary roles in the military, which although not part of the fighting forces are essential to its smooth running. These positions include musicians, standard bearers, camp followers who act as water carriers and servants, and military scribes who are responsible for recording the many successes.

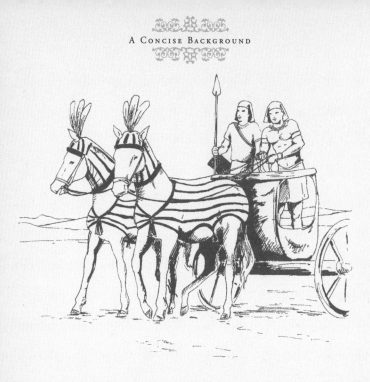

The Egyptian army makes use of the chariot, a weapon of devastating effect, with a driver accompanied by a spearman.

MERCENARIES

For some 2,000 years there have been foreign mercenaries in the Egyptian army, and this hasn't changed in recent times; if anything their numbers have increased since the battle of Kadesh.

Sometimes these men are prisoners of war, who have been given the option of joining the Egyptian army or facing execution, whereas others have joined voluntarily for the perks of the job. Other nationalities that march alongside the Egyptian troops include the Syrians, Libyans, Sherden (identified by their little horned helmets) and Hittites. In the town of Pr-Rameses there are many Hittite soldiers and a workshop for their weapons.

Nubians are the most common mercenaries, often forming corps of archers due to their renowned skill with the bow. However, the Medjay Nubians from the eastern deserts of Nubia have also been used as scouts and light infantry for centuries. So many of this tribe are employed in this occupation that the local police force is referred to simply as the "Medjay."

THE CITY
OF THEBES

*The Theban region is rich in tourist attractions,
and there is something for everyone. However, many
of the temples and tombs are officially closed to
the public, and it requires a great deal of cunning,
and even perhaps bribes, to gain access to some of
these places. With a deep enough purse, however,
nothing is impossible.*

AN OVERVIEW OF THEBES

YOU WILL FIND THEBES ON THE EAST BANK OF THE NILE IN THE SOUTH OF EGYPT. IT HAS A LONG HISTORY, DEVELOPING FROM A SMALL PROVINCIAL TOWN TO THE SPRAWLING METROPOLIS THAT IT IS TODAY. THE LOCAL GOD IS AMUN, WHOSE POPULARITY HAS BECOME WIDESPREAD MEANING THAT HIS TEMPLE AT KARNAK (IPET-SUT) IS THE WEALTHIEST IN EGYPT AND THEBES IS EGYPT'S RELIGIOUS CAPITAL. THEBES REALLY IS A TOWN WITH EVERYTHING AVAILABLE TO ENTERTAIN A VISITOR.

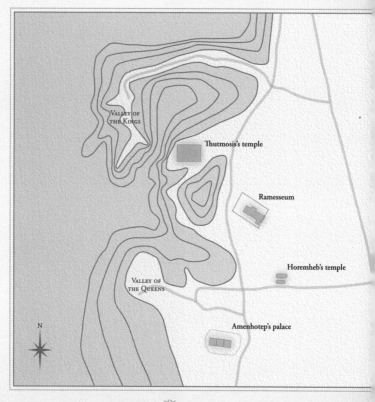

VALLEY OF THE KINGS

Thutmosis's temple

Ramesseum

Horemheb's temple

VALLEY OF THE QUEENS

Amenhotep's palace

N

THE TOWN THAT DOESN'T SLEEP

As a religious capital and the site of the royal cemetery Thebes is a busy metropolis, and has one of the largest populations in Egypt. Therefore you should be aware that there will be crowds of people and the town itself is very noisy. Even at night the noise doesn't stop, but don't despair you may find peace in the Nile's beauty.

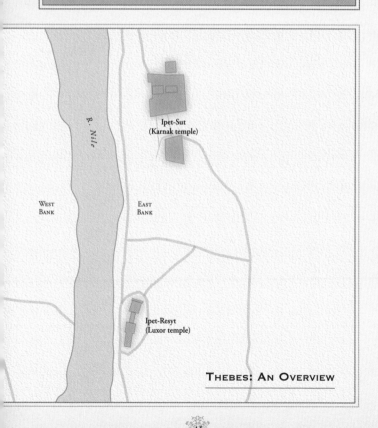

R. Nile

Ipet-Sut
(Karnak temple)

WEST
BANK

EAST
BANK

Ipet-Resyt
(Luxor temple)

THEBES: AN OVERVIEW

THE TEMPLE AT KARNAK

IPET-SUT, OR KARNAK TEMPLE, ON THE EAST BANK OF THE
NILE AT THEBES, IS THE SECOND-LARGEST TEMPLE COMPLEX
IN EGYPT, AND IS DEDICATED TO THE SOLAR DEITY AMUN. THE
TEMPLE IS IN LINE WITH AND CONNECTED TO IPET-RESYT, OR
LUXOR TEMPLE, VIA A LONG AVENUE OF SPHINXES, USED IN
RELIGIOUS PROCESSIONS. AS YOU APPROACH THE TEMPLE,
THE SPHINXES NEAREST THE PYLON HAVE BEEN CONSTRUCTED
BY THE CURRENT KING. AT THE END OF THE AVENUE YOU ARE
GREETED BY A PYLON (MONUMENTAL GATEWAY) LEADING TO
THE GREAT HYPOSTYLE HALL (A PILLARED HALL) BOTH BUILT
BY RAMSES. THE ENTRANCE TO THE HALL IS FLANKED BY
TWO RED GRANITE COLOSSAL STATUES OF RAMSES, MAKING
IT VERY CLEAR THAT THIS IS HIS ENTRANCE.

On the external northern wall of the hypostyle hall are battle reliefs of both Sety and Ramses, both fighting against the Hittites, and on the southern external wall is the Hittite peace treaty signed by Ramses after the battle of Kadesh.

Following the central axis of the temple through the hypostyle hall, the visitor passes through the gateway of Amenhotep Nebmaatra's pylon, with the door inlaid with gold and semiprecious stones, and finds themselves in the central court, which houses the great standing obelisks of Thutmosis Akheperkara and Thutmosis Menkheperre. The visitor then passes through another two pylons built by Thutmosis Akheperkara before arriving at the Hall of Records built by Thutmosis

Menkheperre. It is here that many of the sacred temple texts and records of booty and gifts given to the temple are stored, and these are unlikely to be accessible to even the most affluent of visitors. The final pylon leads to the sanctuary of the temple, housing the shrine within which is the statue of Amun. Only the king and the high priest have access to this chamber.

THE EAR CHAPEL

The ear chapel is possibly the only part of the temple that tourists will have access to. It is situated at the rear of the main Amun temple to the north of the building, near the sanctuary.

The external wall of this chapel is decorated in ear *stelae*—blocks of stone with ears carved on them.

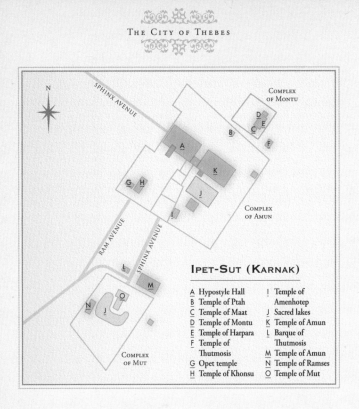

N

SPHINX AVENUE

COMPLEX
OF MONTU

COMPLEX
OF AMUN

RAM AVENUE

SPHINX AVENUE

COMPLEX
OF MUT

IPET-SUT (KARNAK)

A Hypostyle Hall
B Temple of Ptah
C Temple of Maat
D Temple of Montu
E Temple of Harpara
F Temple of
   Thutmosis
G Opet temple
H Temple of Khonsu
I Temple of
   Amenhotep
J Sacred lakes
K Temple of Amun
L Barque of
   Thutmosis
M Temple of Amun
N Temple of Ramses
O Temple of Mut

Pilgrims approach these ears and whisper their prayers and desires into them. It is believed that these prayers go straight into the ears of the god Ptah, the creator deity and patron god of craftsmen.

This chapel at Karnak is in fact quite special, as it is common for the god to respond instantaneously to requests. His voice can be heard instructing the pilgrim on what needs to be done for their request to be granted. These instructions normally involve building a chapel or shrine, or dedicating a statue to the god. Some skeptics may say that this "voice of the god" is actually none other than that of a priest of Karnak—although it would not be fitting to be heard saying this publicly.

The sacred lake represents the primeval waters of Nun.

THE SACRED LAKE

Another area that may be accessible is the sacred lake at Karnak, which is a most beautiful and peaceful place, reminiscent of the primeval waters before creation. This is where the priests purify themselves before entering the temple. The lake was built by Thutmosis Menkheperre and is two-thirds the size of the temple itself. It is located to the south of the temple, near the hypostyle hall. The kitchens are also situated close by, and there are rumors that a tunnel connects the lake to the kitchens and the goose pens. Every now and again one of the geese is let into the lake via this tunnel, appearing on the lake as if from nowhere, symbolizing Amun at creation, demonstrating the still-active creative powers of the lake.

THE HYPOSTYLE HALL

The most impressive part of the temple of Karnak is the great hypostyle hall of Ramses. Planned by the first Ramses, begun by Sety Menmaatra, and completed by Ramses the Great, this hall covers an area of 9,401 square cubits and consists of 134 columns in 16 rows, supporting the roof. The columns along the central axis are taller than the others and stand 39 cubits high; they have floral capitals whereas the others have bud capitals.

From above these columns, high in the ceiling comes the only light in the hall, through stone grills. The hall is therefore dark and shadowy, with only intermittent shafts of light illuminating small areas at a time. The entire hall, including the pillars, is decorated in carved relief. On the northern wall are the beautiful raised relief images of Sety Menmaatra, and on the southern wall the sunk relief of his son. These images of Ramses include his coronation and the role of the gods on this occasion. The pillars themselves are also decorated in polychrome relief, showing the king embracing numerous deities. One solitary pillar, the first in the sixth row, bears the name of the first Ramses, and an eagle-eyed tourist may spot it.

The magnificent hypostyle hall completed by Ramses.

THE OPET FESTIVAL

If you are in Thebes in the second month of the inundation, you may witness the Opet Festival. Lasting 11 days, this Theban holiday is a time of frivolity, new beginnings, and fertility, when crowds fill the streets, hoping to catch a glimpse of the king, or the divine barque.

The festivities start when the statue of Amun is carried in procession from Karnak to Luxor temple along the sphinx avenue, a distance of 3,846 cubits. This part of the procession is invisible to the public, as the ceremonial way is hidden by large enclosure walls, but the noise of the accompanying singers and musicians can still be heard.

The return journey is by river, and is a far more public event. The divine barque bearing the statue of the god is towed by a small flotilla of sailing boats accompanied by the royal barge, itself towed by the military as they run along the banks of the Nile. Although the soldiers may restrict the view, it may be possible to catch a glimpse of the king as he sits upon his barge.

THE COMPLEX OF MUT

The complex of Mut lies to the far south of the Karnak complex. It is reached from the southern gate via a sphinx avenue. To the east of the sphinx avenue is a small temple to Amun-Kamutef, and on the western side is a barque shrine built by Thutmosis Menkheperre as a resting point during processions.

The temple has two open courtyards, and a sanctuary surrounded by antechambers; but the main temple is unusual as it is surrounded on three sides by a horseshoe-shaped lake.

A point of interest is the chapel of Sekhmet, filled with hundreds of life-sized black granite statues of the goddess. Sekhmet is the goddess of war, plagues, and epidemics, and it is thought that Amenhotep commissioned so many statues of her due to suffering in his later years from ill health.

To the north of the enclosure is a small temple dedicated to the child of Mut and Amun, Khonsu, displaying some interesting divine birth scenes and one of only two images in Egypt of a circumcision ceremony.

THE TEMPLE OF LUXOR

THE TEMPLE OF LUXOR AT THEBES (KNOWN LOCALLY AS AMENEMOPET—"AMUN OF OPET"), IS SMALLER THAN KARNAK BUT NO LESS IMPRESSIVE, AND THE TWO ARE CONNECTED BY A CEREMONIAL WAY. THIS FOR MANY YEARS WAS A CANAL FILLED WITH WATER FROM THE NILE, ALLOWING THE SACRED BARK BEARING THE STATUE OF THE GOD TO SAIL BETWEEN THE TWO TEMPLES. IN RECENT YEARS THE FLOODS HAVE NOT BEEN SUFFICIENT TO REACH THIS CANAL, SO IT IS BEING MADE INTO A SPHINX AVENUE. THIS PROCESSIONAL WAY IS USED DURING THE OPET FESTIVAL WHEN THE GOD AMUN TRAVELS FROM KARNAK TO LUXOR TEMPLE.

The temple of Luxor itself is primarily the temple of Amenhotep Nebmaatra, although it stands on the site of a smaller temple to the god Amun built over 700 years ago. However, all visitors to the temple are greeted by the marvellous pylon gateway built by the current ruler Ramses Usermaatra-Setepenra. In front of the pylon are six colossal granite statues of the king, two seated and four standing, and two huge obelisks 47 cubits high—leaving the visitor in no doubt as to who built this gateway, and also giving the false impression that he built the entire temple.

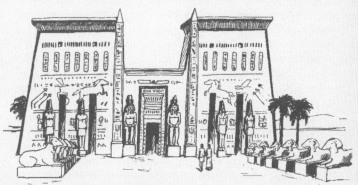

The imposing façade of the temple of Luxor. Note the colossal granite statues of Ramses flanking the gateway.

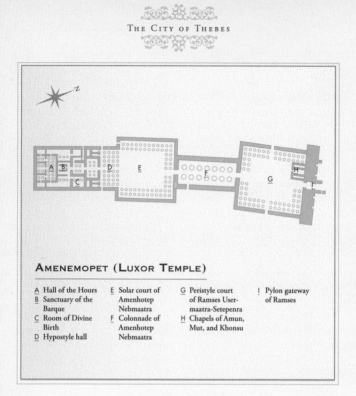

AMENEMOPET (LUXOR TEMPLE)

A Hall of the Hours
B Sanctuary of the
  Barque
C Room of Divine
  Birth
D Hypostyle hall

E Solar court of
  Amenhotep
  Nebmaatra
F Colonnade of
  Amenhotep
  Nebmaatra

G Peristyle court
  of Ramses User-
  maatra-Setepenra
H Chapels of Amun,
  Mut, and Khonsu

I Pylon gateway
  of Ramses

As is traditional, the pylon is decorated with battle scenes, primarily Ramses' victory against the Hittites at Kadesh in year 5 of his reign. These types of images intimidate anyone who plans to cause harm to the Egyptians or to the temple itself. If you are allowed to enter the temple through the enormous wooden doors, you will yourself in the colonnaded courtyard of Ramses with 74 columns. Between the first row of columns to the south are more colossal statues of Ramses, as well as a stunning dyad of Ramses and Nefertari, his Great Royal Wife, depicted as Amun and Mut. Within this courtyard are three small chapels dedicated to the Theban triad, Amun, Mut and their child Khonsu. Originally this was built by Thutmosis Menkheperre, but the current king Ramses has adopted them for his own. They are used during the Opet festival for the statue of Amun to receive refreshment on his journey. These shrines were originally more central in the courtyard, but Ramses moved them closer to the northwestern wall.

The walls of this colonnade are decorated with polychrome scenes of Ramses making offerings to the gods, as well as images of his wives and children. This is a unique insight into the royal family, not generally visible to outsiders. However, it is possible, if one is wealthy enough, to commission a statue of oneself and have it placed within this courtyard in the presence of the god and the rituals at all times. Even if you can't access this temple, it is possible for your statue to be dedicated by a priest for a small fee.

THE WORK OF AMENHOTEP

Continuing through the temple, the visitor is confronted by the earlier structures of Amenhotep, starting with the colonnade bearing seven pairs of columns. This was intended to be the entrance when it was originally built. It is a compact, dark area with only small windows high up in the walls providing light, which makes for a marked contrast with the bright openness of the first court.

Although the colonnade is of Amenhotep Nebmaatra's design, the decoration was added by Horemheb and Sety Menmaatra. The columns are adorned with images of the Opet Festival celebrated at Luxor and Karnak. This colonnade is on an axis with the temple of Khonsu at Karnak, and joined to it by another ceremonial way.

Traversing the colonnade, the visitor will enter Amenhotep's solar court, which is another colonnaded courtyard with two rows of 60 pillars surrounding the walls. These walls are decorated with images of Amenhotep and the god Amun. Then you enter the hypostyle hall, which was repaired by the father of the current king, Sety Menmaatra. There are 32 papyrus columns, and the walls are decorated with images of Amenhotep making various offerings to the god Amun.

Leading off the hypostyle hall are a number of chambers, chapels, and vestibules with many different functions. Two of particular interest to the visitor are the Room of Divine Birth, depicting the divine conception and birth of Amenhotep, and the offering vestibule displaying an image of Amenhotep leading fattened cattle to the temple to be slaughtered for Amun.

A depiction of fattened cattle being offered to Amun.

THE PYLON OF RAMSES

As you approach the pylon of the current king Ramses Usermaatra-Setepenra at Luxor temple, you will see the elaborate and colorful images of the so-called victory of Ramses at Kadesh back in year 5 of his reign.

The expedition to Kadesh was launched from the city of Pr-Rameses in the Delta. There were four military divisions, with the Amun division led by the king himself. Three Egyptian divisions camped just outside the town, and scouts captured two Hittite spies. Unfortunately they lied to the king and informed him that the Hittites had fled in fear, when in reality they were waiting in ambush.

The Egyptians continued to the fortified town, only to be attacked by the Hittites lying in wait. The Amun division were so surprised they fled the way that they had come, with the Hittites following them. The fourth Egyptian division arrived sometime later, surprising the Hittites who fled into their fortified town. The Egyptians laid siege to Kadesh, but they were unable to penetrate the walls. They eventually returned to Egypt in "victory." Ramses has since recorded this victory at Kadesh in eight places.

THE BIRTH OF AMENHOTEP NEBMAATRA

There are a number of side-rooms off the hypostyle hall at Luxor temple, and one of them bears the most interesting imagery of the divine conception and birth of King Amenhotep Nebmaatra.

The images start with the conception of queen Mutemwia, Amenhotep's mother, by the god Amun. Amenhotep's body and his *ka* (spirit) are depicted being created on a potter's wheel by the ram-headed god Khnum, overseen by the goddess Isis. Isis embraces the queen, as Djehuty (the god of wisdom) leads Amun to the bedchamber of the queen. His presence is announced by the scent of incense, the body-odor of the god. The child and his ka, already prepared, are placed in the womb of the queen, and the birth is aided by Bes and Taweret, the deities of childbirth, ensuring that the divinity of the king is under no question. The king is then suckled by the deities and presented to Amun by Horus.

THE TEMPLES OF THUTMOSIS MENKHEPERRE AND MENTUHOTEP NEBHETEPRE

TO THE SOUTH OF THE MORTUARY TEMPLE OF THE CURRENT KING IS THE VALLEY HOUSING THE TEMPLES OF THUTMOSIS MENKHEPERRE AND MENTUHOTEP NEBHETEPRE. THUTMOSIS BUILT HIS TEMPLE HIGH IN THE CLIFF FACE, BUT DID NOT LIVE TO SEE ITS COMPLETION. DUE TO ITS ELEVATION IT IS POSSIBLE TO SEE THIS BEAUTIFUL TEMPLE FROM THE EAST BANK OF THE NILE ON A CLEAR DAY.

The temple consists of three terraces, each joined by ramps flanked by porticoes on either side; all decorated in carved and painted relief. Sadly, as the temple and approach ramps were built over the remains of Mentuhotep's temple, it is difficult to identify elements from this earlier structure, although some pillars still stand and the roof supports the weight of the newer monument above. The rear wall of the lower terrace of Thutmosis' temple is in fact built in front of Mentuhotep's temple, obscuring it from view, although the adventurous tourist could perhaps explore a little.

The temple of Thutmosis is approached by a long, tree-lined

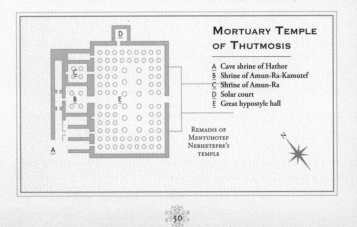

MORTUARY TEMPLE OF THUTMOSIS

A Cave shrine of Hathor
B Shrine of Amun-Ra-Kamutef
C Shrine of Amun-Ra
D Solar court
E Great hypostyle hall

REMAINS OF MENTUHOTEP NEBHETEPRE'S TEMPLE

causeway, and just at the entrance to the valley is a way-station that provides a temporary home for the sacred statue of the king or god during long processions. This causeway is impressive at 63 cubits, 3 palms, and 2 fingers wide, made of shining limestone. As the causeway is surrounded by enclosure walls it is not usually possible to walk along it, but on non-festival days a few "greased palms" may go a long way.

The sacred cow of Hathor looms out of its small shrine.

GODS OF THE TEMPLE

The main gods worshipped at the temple are Amun-Ra and Amun-Ra-Kamutef, both royal deities—although there is a small cave shrine to Hathor just behind the northern corner of Mentuhotep's temple. A visit to this part of the site is strongly recommended. It is a small, decorated vaulted chamber dominated by a full-size statue of Hathor in cow form. At the rear is a kneeling figure of Amenhotep Akheperure, who dedicated the shrine, suckling from the sacred cow, and a standing figure of the same king under Hathor's chin. The shrine still functions, and it is possible to leave offerings.

Above this shrine the genius of Thutmosis' builders can be seen: a false platform was created, projecting out of the cliff face, to level and enlarge a natural outcrop upon which the main temple is constructed. This forms the upper level of the three terraces and houses a large hypostyle hall of 32 columns, with a small kiosk in the center. There are a number of rooms leading from this hall, including a shrine to Amun-Ra, one to Amun-Ra-Kamutef, and a small, open-roofed solar chapel. All of the rooms and the hypostyle hall are highly decorated with scenes of the king making offerings to Amun, and beautiful images of the god in his sacred barque on procession during the Beautiful Festival of the Valley held annually on the Theban west bank.

To reach this terrace from ground level, one needs to ascend a ramp 100 cubits long that rises 38 cubits, 3 palms, and 2 fingers. Although difficult to reach, if the opportunity arises to visit this temple it is wholeheartedly recommended.

THE TEMPLE OF
AMENHOTEP NEBMAATRA

THE MORTUARY TEMPLE OF AMENHOTEP NEBMAATRA (INSET) ON THE WEST BANK OF THE NILE IS ONE OF THE BIGGEST AND MOST BEAUTIFUL TEMPLES IN EGYPT, ALTHOUGH IN RECENT YEARS THE SITE HAS BEEN QUARRIED FOR STONE TO BUILD THE LATER MONUMENTS ON THE WEST BANK.

The first temple gateway is flanked by two colossal seated statues of the king that stand 34 cubits tall. Smaller images of his wife Tiye and his mother Mutemwia stand at his feet.

The stone for these statues was quarried far in the north of Egypt, at the Red Mountain near Iunu—a great feat in itself. In addition to these two colossal statues, Amenhotep built a great number of other statues within the temple, including four massive statues in front of two further pylons. Each of these statues has details picked out in blue, red, green, yellow, and white, and the pylons themselves are highly decorated with colored murals of the king smiting his enemies. Each of the pylons was once adorned with flags atop golden poles, but these were among the first things removed when the temple fell into disuse.

Between the first and second and the second and third pylons are two large, open courts. Behind the third pylon is a long processional corridor, in a similar manner to that of the same king at Luxor temple. This corridor leads to a large solar court, open in the center, with three rows of columns to the east, west, and south of the court and four rows at the north of the court.

THE SOLAR COURT
AND BEYOND

The entrance to the solar court is flanked by two large *stelae* outlining the building achievements of the king. Between each of these papyriform pillars stand colossal statues of the king as Osiris, showing that the dead king is to be worshipped here. This area is also used as a sed-festival hall, and it is here that every 30 years the king proves his virility and his ability to rule Egypt. In a funerary context this ensures he will live forever in the afterlife as a king.

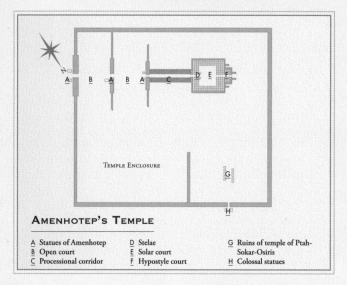

AMENHOTEP'S TEMPLE

TEMPLE ENCLOSURE

A Statues of Amenhotep
B Open court
C Processional corridor
D Stelae
E Solar court
F Hypostyle court
G Ruins of temple of Ptah-
   Sokar-Osiris
H Colossal statues

Along the eastern wall of the temple are over 70 life-sized statues of the goddess of plagues and epidemics, Sekhmet, carved from black granite and placed here by the king in a bid for good health. At Karnak's temple of Mut there are also hundreds of these statues—thought to be the old king's last hope against ill health.

In the north of the court a door in the center leads to a small hypostyle hall before you reach the sanctuary at the rear, which is built upon a small raised mound. It is best to visit this temple during the months of flood, as the temple is built on the floodplain and the whole area floods during this time, with nothing but the sanctuary

being left dry; reminiscent of the mound of creation rising from the primeval waters.

In the northern part of the enclosure are remains of another small temple dedicated to Ptah-Sokar-Osiris, with two colossal statues outside the enclosure walls flanking the gateway. This small temple is built from local limestone and is a major part of the funerary cult. Sadly, there is little of this temple remaining. The rest of the mortuary temple also is in a ruinous state, and it is therefore one of the few temples that can be entered freely by the tourist, as it is no longer filled with priests and has long since been neglected by the Medjay.

THE PALACE AT MALKATA

IF THERE IS A DONKEY AVAILABLE WHEN YOU ARE ON THE WEST BANK, WHY NOT TRAVEL SOUTH PAST THE MORTUARY TEMPLE OF HOREMHEB TO THE PALACE OF THE GREAT AMENHOTEP NEBMAATRA? AS IT IS NO LONGER INHABITED, THE BUILDING MATERIAL IS BEING REUSED FOR OTHER CONSTRUCTION WORK, BUT THERE IS STILL ENOUGH TO SEE TO MAKE IT WORTHWHILE.

To refer to the "Splendor of the Aten" as a palace is a bit of a misnomer, as in its heyday it was a huge city. There was even a causeway leading to the mortuary temple of Amenhotep further north, and the adventurous tourist could walk this causeway.

The whole city was constructed of mud brick, and those areas of the site that were not plundered for this valuable material have been damaged by a recent rainstorm. The city itself is organized well, with a combination of royal and official residences. The north village housed the supplies needed for running the city; the south village contained the workshops and faience factories, and also a separate area for the servant quarters.

The northern palace belonged to the daughter and wife of Amenhotep; Sitamun, the Middle Palace, belonged to the king; and the south palace belonged to the Great Royal Wife, Tiye.

The pavements throughout the palace areas were elaborately decorated with colored tiles depicting scenes of wildlife, as well as more traditional scenes of the enemies of the king being trampled underfoot. One of the most beautiful floors shows a colorful marsh scene complete with swimming ducks, fish and geese, almost a replica of the beautiful views to be seen from the pleasure lake in the grounds, and is still visible amidst the sand.

THE ROYAL PALACE

The royal palace, called the "House of Rejoicing," is particularly beautiful, and in its day was glorious. The palace is a single-story structure with a number of rooms open to the sky, allowing the warm sun and cool breezes into the living quarters. The outside of the palace was painted white, with blue faience inlays displaying hieroglyphic inscriptions, some of which are still visible.

Inside the palace there are numerous small audience chambers, all highly decorated. Most decoration within the palace is geometric or naturalistic; however, there are exceptions and in one of the audience chambers are beautiful images of dancing girls, and even a stunning scene of the king hunting. The pavement leading to his throne bore designs of captive Asiatics, Nubians, and the *nine bows*, representing the king's superiority over these enemies of Egypt.

The banqueting hall is most impressive, note the elaborate decoration at the king's end, compared to the plainer end.

Whilst visiting the ruined palace take the opportunity to visit the harem and the kings bedroom—a once-in-a-lifetime experience.

The harem consists of four suites of rooms on either side of the banqueting hall, each with four chambers, which acted as living quarters, sleeping quarters and the bathrooms for the royal ladies. Obviously this did not house all 1,000 ladies of Amenhotep's harem, just the favored few on a temporary basis. The king's bedchamber had the thickest walls in the palace, and were decorated with protective hieroglyphs to aid in the protection and fertility of the king.

WHAT TO EXPECT

AMENHOTEP'S PLEASURE LAKE

Just south of the palace of Amenhotep is an artificial lake that the king excavated for his chief wife Tiye. This huge T-shaped lake is attached to the Nile.

The king was so proud of his achievement that he commissioned a number of commemorative scarabs recording the 15-day excavation. There must have been a great number of men working on the site, and you can still see the displaced soil in artificial mounds around the lake.

As this lake is filled by the Nile, it is also filled with fish and wildlife, and is more than big enough to accommodate a boat. So before you arrive at the site arrange for a boatman on the Nile to meet you here for a pleasant afternoon's rowing on the royal lake.

THE RAMESSEUM
(OR KHNEMET-WASET)

THE TEMPLE OF MILLIONS OF YEARS OF THE CURRENT KING IS SITUATED ON THE WEST BANK AT THEBES AND IS ONE OF THE MOST VIBRANT INSTITUTIONS IN THE CITY. ALTHOUGH A MORTUARY TEMPLE, IT IS ALREADY IN USE IN RAMSES' LIFETIME. IT TOOK 20 YEARS TO COMPLETE. THIS LARGE COMPLEX OF TWO TEMPLES, A PALACE, AND NUMEROUS ADMINISTRATIVE BUILDINGS AND MAGAZINES IS APPROACHED BY AVENUES OF SPHINXES, USED FOR PROCESSIONS OF THE STATUE OF THE KING.

This is the most impressive of all Ramses' structures and includes the first stone pylon in Egypt and also the largest statue ever built. This statue is of granite from the quarries at Aswan, and it was no mean feat getting the block to Thebes in one piece.

THE MAIN TEMPLE

The main temple is oriented so that its pylons face those of Luxor temple, and is built to line up with a temple dedicated to Ramses' mother Tuya to the east of the hypostyle hall.

The main temple consists of a stone pylon gateway decorated with scenes of the famous battle of Kadesh, followed by an open courtyard. The focus of this court is the colossal statue of the king, flanked on both sides by his mother Tuya.

A door in the west wall leads to a peristyle court, with a colonnade around the outside and open in the center. Each of the pillars on the eastern and western walls are constructed of statues of the king as Osiris. Between these pillars the king has set up further colossal statues of himself.

The northern wall of this court also bears images from the battle of Kadesh, showing the victory of the king for eternity. There is also a detailed rendering of the fertility festival of Min, where the statue of the god is carried in procession and worshipped by the king. This festival took place at Ramses' coronation and is remembered by many older Theban residents.

At the rear of the first court the king is depicted with eleven of his sons, all of whom have sadly passed on since the temple was built.

THE HYPOSTYLE HALLS

Continuing along the central axis leads to the hypostyle hall, somewhat less impressive than Ramses' hall at Karnak, but still of a monumental scale. Lit by small windows high up in the roof, it is supported by 48 papyriform columns. The walls surrounding the hypostyle hall are highly decorated with images of the king before various gods, including a wonderful scene showing the coronation of the king, where his name is being written on the sacred tree of Iunu by the god Atum as the deities of writing and intelligence, Thoth and Seshat, stand by. Other scenes show his military victories, those at the Asiatic town of Zapur being most worthy of note.

The most impressive of Ramses' monuments—his mortuary temple.

At the rear of the main hypostyle hall are three smaller courts before you reach the barque shrine which houses the cult statue of the king at the rear.

In the first of these smaller courts is an astronomical ceiling displaying the constellations of the stars and the divisions of the night sky, painted in vibrant colors with gilding picking out the details. There are further astronomical reliefs on the eastern wall. This hall is used primarily as a library, and the archives are kept here.

AROUND THE TEMPLE

As at most temples there is a sacred lake here, within which the priests purify themselves before entering the temple. Don't be tempted to swim in it—the punishment for non-temple personnel found taking a dip is death.

To the west of the first court is the palace of Ramses, which is used for temporary accommodation during festivals when the king is to carry out rituals within the temple. There is a well to the west which serves the palace.

To the east of the temple is a small birth house that celebrates the divine birth of Ramses. On three sides of the temple, outside the walls, are many storage magazines and administrative buildings that store and distribute rations of grain and other foodstuffs to those within the royal employ.

At harvest time the magazines are filled with grain through the holes in the top of their structures. These magazines are all made of mud brick and have domed ceilings; they are quite interesting to see, even though entering them is out of the question.

THE CHAPEL OF
THE WHITE QUEEN

ONCE YOU HAVE FINISHED VISITING THE MORTUARY TEMPLE OF RAMSES, A SHORT DISTANCE NORTH YOU WILL DISCOVER THE SMALL "CHAPEL OF THE WHITE QUEEN." THIS IS NAMED AFTER ITS BEAUTIFUL LIMESTONE STATUE OF MERITAMUN, THE BELOVED DAUGHTER OF THE CURRENT KING RAMSES, IN HER ROLE AS "SISTRUM (RATTLE) PLAYER OF MUT" AND "DANCER OF HORUS."

The site itself has been sacred for over 700 years, and tombs in this area are scattered around the hills and valley floor. Although it is probably inaccessible to the tourist, it might just be possible to view some of the carved decoration in the courtyard, and also to leave some small tokens of respect in this open area.

The chapel, as it stands, was built by the heretic king, but was strangely enough not destroyed with the others from his reign, although certain elements can be dated to the earlier reign of Amenhotep Akheperre, and some kitchen buildings still produce food for the festivals on the west bank.

Although abandoned after the reign of the heretic king, it has since been added to by Ramses, and the enclosure wall of his mortuary temple abuts its western wall.

The beautiful limestone statue of Meritamun, daughter of Ramses, for which the Chapel of the White Queen is named.

WITHIN THE CHAPEL

One may approach the temple by road, although a more scenic route would be to enter through the harbor. Once you leave your boat, approach a ramp leading to the first of two limestone entrance pylons. As this is a royal chapel it is not open to the public, but once you reach the huge wooden door, it may be possible to pay the doorman to let you peek at the temple enclosure behind.

Beyond the pylons, you will see within the enclosure walls two identical structures consisting of two small rooms, each joined by a long walled corridor. In front of each is a large courtyard.

A more traditional chapel can be found near these two buildings, consisting of three small chambers which accommodate the divine triad, the god, his consort and their child. Here is the main hub of the temple, where priests make daily offerings, and it is possible for the visitor to leave an offering with the priests who will place it before the god on your behalf.

WHAT TO EXPECT

THE TEMPLE OF WADJMOSE

If you are ready to see the exterior walls of more chapels in the area, just to the south of the mortuary temple of Ramses and the Chapel of the White Queen is the small temple of Wadjmose, the son of Thutmosis Akheperkara. This prince died at a young age, and this temple was built in his honor by his family.

The temple complex is approached by a sphinx avenue. Within the enclosure walls are two courtyards, the second housing three sanctuaries which occupy the whole rear of the monument. The central sanctuary was for the worship of Wadjmose, the northern for his mother Mutneferet, and the southern houses the oracle. Wadjmose has been approached for centuries as an oracle, to advise on various matters, although this is seen as rather unfashionable now and is less popular than it has been in the past.

THE VALLEY OF THE KINGS

THE VALLEY OF THE KINGS, KNOWN LOCALLY AS THE "GREAT NOBLE NECROPOLIS OF MILLIONS OF YEARS OF THE KING" WAS THE BURIAL GROUND FOR OVER 60 KINGS OF THE LAST THREE CENTURIES. THE BURIAL GROUND IS SITUATED ON THE WEST BANK OF THE NILE, AND OF THE TWO VALLEYS THE MAJORITY OF THE TOMBS ARE IN THE WESTERN VALLEY.

The cliffs surrounding the valley are patrolled by the Medjay and guardposts atop the cliffs provide panoramic views. The site was chosen because of one of the mountains at the southern end, which looks like a pyramid and is referred to as Meretseger, in reference to a local goddess ("She Who Loves Silence") who is believed to protect the valley.

JOURNEY OF THE SUN-GOD

There are over 50 tombs in the necropolis, and most of them follow a similar structure based on the journey of the sun-god. The basic elements are:

The Passage of the Way of Shu—the entrance into the tomb.

The Passage of Ra—a long corridor, the beginning of which is still reached by the rays of the sun.

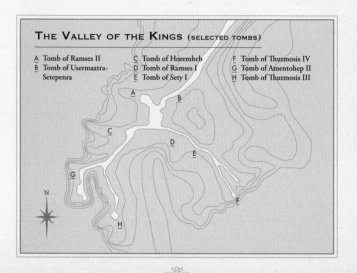

THE VALLEY OF THE KINGS (SELECTED TOMBS)

A Tomb of Ramses II
B Tomb of Usermaatra-Setepenra
C Tomb of Horemheb
D Tomb of Ramses I
E Tomb of Sety I
F Tomb of Thutmosis IV
G Tomb of Amentohep II
H Tomb of Thutmosis III

The Hall Where the Gods of the Litany of Ra Reside—a small chamber or corridor reached by a short staircase or ramp.

The Hall of Hindering—this is a deep well chamber that acts as a deterrent to robbers, as well as being a symbolic burial of Osiris

The Chariot Hall—a pillared chamber.

There are often other corridors and chambers as well leading to the "Hall in Which One Rests," or burial chamber.

Each of these is elaborately decorated, either in carved relief or painted plaster. The decoration comprises vignettes from the *Book of the Dead*, the *Book of Gates* or the *Litany of Re*, which all deal with the nocturnal journey of the sun-god Ra, and by association the journey of the dead king.

The natural pyramid of Meretsegar, "She Who Loves Silence."

ENTRY TO THE VALLEY

It is highly unlikely that tourists will gain access to any of the tombs in the "Great Noble Necropolis of Millions of Years of the King," and indeed the Medjay may prevent access to the Valley altogether. That said, the tomb of the sons of Ramses is still being constructed and opened for royal burials.

THE TOMB OF USERMAATRA-SETEPENRA

One of the newest additions to the Valley of the Kings is the tomb built for the sons of Ramses Usermaatra-Setepenra. It is situated at the entrance to the valley, on the left-hand side, with the entrance concealed at the bottom of the cliff.

Rumors have it that there are over 130 burial chambers in the tomb, all leading from long corridors, each designed to accommodate the burial of a son or grandchild of Ramses. So far twelve princes have been buried within the tomb. Each of the chambers is carved and painted with elaborate offering scenes and vignettes from the *Book of the Dead*, and *Book of the Gates*, as well as images of the princes themselves entering the afterlife. Although there is little chance of a visitor gaining access to this royal sepulcher, it is worth knowing where it is and what is inside.

THE VALLEY OF THE QUEENS

THE VALLEY OF THE QUEENS OR "TA SET NEFERU" (PLACE OF THE BEAUTEOUS ONES) IS THE BURIAL PLACE FOR THE ROYAL WOMEN AND CHILDREN—A TWIN TO THE VALLEY OF THE KINGS IT IS SITUATED 2,830 CUBITS SOUTHWEST OF THERE. THIS AREA WAS CHOSEN FOR ITS GEOGRAPHY; IT IS A U-SHAPED VALLEY, WITH A SMALL CAVE AT THE BOTTOM OF THE CLIFF THAT FILLS WITH WATER WHEN IT RAINS. THESE WATERS THEN FLOOD THE VALLEY, REPRESENTING THE WOMB OF HATHOR, FROM WHICH THE DECEASED CAN BE REBORN.

However, this relatively recent addition to the west bank was initiated just 300 years ago. Prior to that the royal women were buried with their husbands in the kings' tombs.

There are over 50 tombs in the Place of the Beauteous Ones, although a number of them are unfinished and undecorated—some being little more than a small cave carved into the desert floor.

EARLY BURIALS

The earliest tomb here belongs to Ahmose—the daughter of King Seqenenre Tao and sister of King Ahmose, who expelled the hated Heqa Haswt from Egypt around 300 years ago.

Although there have been other burials here since that of Ahmose, the names of these queens have long since been forgotten, up until the burial of Satra, the wife of the first Ramses, the grandfather of the current king.

CHILDREN OF RAMSES

During the last 50 years of the reign of the current Ramses there have been a number of royal funerals, and at least three of his royal daughters are buried here: Bintanath, Meritamun, Nebtawy, as well as his eldest son Ramses. All the other sons of Ramses are buried in the tomb built for them in the Valley of the Kings.

All the tombs from the modern era are elaborately built with pillared halls, stairways, and corridors; whereas the earlier ones are simpler in design, with a corridor leading to the burial chamber or a simple pit burial.

THE TOMB OF NEFERTARI

The most impressive tomb in the Place of the Beauteous Ones is that of Nefertari, the Great Royal Wife of Ramses, who was laid to rest in her tomb in year 24 of the current king's reign.

She was mourned greatly and hers was the first tomb built for a queen of this reign in the Valley of the Queens.

Unfortunately for the visitor there is absolutely no chance of gaining access, but it may be possible to get to the valley and leave offerings and prayers at the tomb entrance—which is still just about visible.

It is rumored that the internal decoration of the tomb is the most beautiful in all of Egypt, a reflection of the great love that Ramses held for Nefertari. It is traditional that the tombs have colorful vignettes from the *Book of the Dead* and *Book of Gates*, and it is these that provide guidance for the deceased queen once she passed into the afterlife. This tomb was completed by the workmen living at the Place of Truth, who

A depiction of Nefertari, the Great Royal Wife from her tomb.

specialize in colorful finely drawn images and hieroglyphs, and as a royal tomb hers will be of the highest standard.

LOCAL TOMB PAINTINGS

TOMB ART IN NON-ROYAL TOMBS IS VIBRANT AND DYNAMIC AND NO TWO TOMBS ARE ALIKE. THERE ARE, HOWEVER, STOCK THEMES THAT ARE USED: FOOD PROVISION, EVERYDAY LIFE, AND FERTILITY. MOST TOMB IMAGES FALL INTO ONE OF THESE CATEGORIES.

The easiest way of ensuring plenty of food in the afterlife is to paint or carve images on the tomb walls of servants carrying armfuls of food to already full offering tables. These can be seen in virtually every tomb. Many tombs go one step further, with images of food being produced. Therefore there are numerous scenes of fishermen at work, hunters catching birds, bakeries, and breweries. These images ensure the deceased is always provided for in the afterlife.

These images also crossover into the category of everyday life, should the tomb owner be concerned with these industries in his day-to-day work. Many tombs have elaborate scenes of workshops in action, with the tomb owner overseeing the activities that vary from military training to jewelry making. Some images also show the deceased with his family.

This latter theme also crosses over with the third category of artwork, as the deceased's family will help ensure his fertility in the afterlife. Likewise, the common fishing and fowling scenes are a perfect example of this dual meaning as the tomb owner is shown on a family trip in the marshes, an activity that presents him as physically fit, fertile, and boasting great prowess.

The painter of a royal tomb goes about his work.

ROYAL TOMBS

Royal tombs have a completely different collection of images on their tomb walls, and there are stricter guidelines which need to be adhered to when choosing these images. Most royal tombs are decorated with vignettes from funerary texts, which aid the occupant in the afterlife. The most common are the *Book of the Amduat*, the *Book of Gates*, and the *Book of Caverns*.

The *Spells for Going Forth By Day* (or the *Book of the Dead*), are particularly common in both royal and non-royal tombs, and comprise 189 spells based on the older Coffin and Pyramid Texts, some of which should be written on particular objects and materials. The most important spell from this funerary text is NO.125, the "Judgment of the Dead," which includes the weighing of the heart and the negative confession.

The *Book of the Amduat* and the *Book of Gates* both outline the 12-hour nocturnal journey of the sun god. Each hour is separated by a portal guarded by a demon, and often it is these that are depicted on tomb walls. The sun god travels throughout the 12 hours upon a solar barque, accompanied by his entourage; he is the ram-headed deity in the center.

As he is reborn into the world at the end of the 12 hours, and transforms into the scarab beetle, representing the sun-god at dawn. Some images show the sky goddess Nut swallowing the sun at dusk, and giving birth to him at dawn.

From the reign of Thutmosis Menkheperre the *Litany of Re* was introduced, and the father of the current king, Sety, placed it in the entrance corridor of his tomb. It is thought Ramses has done the same. The *Litany of Re* shows the sun god in all 75 forms, many connecting him with other deities to show the sun as the key to all life, and also to emphasize the solar connection with the king.

ARTISTS' TOOLS

The artists who create such works of art do so with the simplest of tools. Paintbrushes are made using a reed, the end of which is frayed and folded over, with the ends firmly tied to the shaft to create a loop at the end. This loop is cut creating a brush.

The paints themselves are made from pigments, ground down into a fine powder which is mixed with a water-soluble gum. Each color is made up only as and when it is needed, and as some colors are more expensive than others these are used sparingly.

WILDLIFE WALKS ALONG THE NILE

ONCE YOU HAVE BEEN SATURATED BY THE CULTURE AND ARCHITECTURE OF THE THEBAN REGION, WHY NOT TAKE A SHORT PLEASURE WALK ALONG THE NILE AND ENJOY THE ABUNDANCE OF WILDLIFE THAT LIVES IN THE WATER AND THE MARSHES? IT IS WORTH NOTING THAT SOME OF THE WILDLIFE ON SHOW CAN BE DANGEROUS, BUT IT SHOULD BE ENTIRELY POSSIBLE TO OBSERVE FROM A SAFE DISTANCE ABOARD A BOAT OR HIDDEN IN THE MARSHES.

The most dangerous creatures in the Nile are its famous crocodiles, and it needs to be noted that they also hide in the marshes and are the biggest killer in Egypt. The second most dangerous animal is the hippopotamus that can regularly be seen wallowing in the shallows. They are generally peaceful but should they be disturbed, especially when there are young close by, they can turn quite vicious and are even capable of killing a crocodile.

The threatening gape of the Nile crocodile.

BIRDS AND INSECTS

If you would like to see something a little less dangerous then the marshes are the place to go, especially if you are interested in birds and insects.

Those that you can expect to see include the Egyptian hoopoe and the pied kingfisher, which builds its nests among the reeds. If you are particularly lucky you may even see mongooses sneaking up to steal its eggs.

Other birds to watch out for include the ibis, sacred to the god Thoth, and the hawk, sacred to the god Horus. To see one of these

The pied kingfisher.

The Egyptian hoopoe.

birds in flight is not just a grand sight, but is also considered to be a fortunate omen.

Alongside the birdlife flutter butterflies and dragonflies, while the cacophony of croaking frogs and chirruping grasshoppers is unrelenting, even when they themselves remain obscured among the reeds.

FISH

In the Nile itself swim a great abundance of fish, and there are always many fishermen to be seen catching fish in their dragnets. However, if a fisherman captures a Nile catfish he will immediately throw it back, as it is associated with the fertility of Osiris and it would be very bad luck indeed to kill it and eat it.

Among the more common fish that are eaten are the built, carp, and electric eel, and they are indeed beautiful to see swimming in their natural habitat.

The sacred Nile catfish.

SURROUNDING AREAS

Although there is more than enough in Thebes to keep even the most active visitor busy, the rest of Egypt also has plenty to offer, from cosmopolitan cities and busy trading harbors to small temples. Whether it is an active weekend or a religious retreat that you are looking for, Egypt has it all.

Egypt is divided into three regions: Lower and Upper Egypt, and Nubia. North or Lower Egypt covers the Delta from the Great Green (Mediterranean Sea) down to Mennefer, including the city of Pr-Rameses and the pyramid fields of Giza and Saqqara. South or Upper Egypt begins at Mennefer and continues south to Nubia, which itself extends further south still.

THE CAPITAL OF PR-RAMESES

WHILE YOU ARE IN THE NORTH OF EGYPT, WHY NOT VISIT THE ROYAL CITY OF PR-RAMESES, THE CITY PERFECTED BY THE CURRENT KING. THE CITY IS IN THE EASTERN DELTA, AND CAN BE REACHED BY WATERWAY FROM THE LAKES OF HORUS, OR BY THE HORUS ROAD FROM THE SINAI. IT IS SITUATED UPON TWO MOUNDS, SURROUNDED BY MARSHLAND THAT OFFERS MARVELOUS FISHING AND FOWLING.

Although an ancient harbor city, Pr-Rameses has been given a recent overhaul and Ramses intends it to rival Thebes as far as beauty and architecture go.

The city is a popular one and many people have moved here from all over Egypt. In the streets of the city, especially in the center of town near the palace, don't be surprised if you spot people of note: royal princes, the vizier, or royal officials such as the king's scribe, or even the commander of the army—a virtual *Who's Who* of the Ramesside court.

WHAT TO SEE

The town has a large military presence—both the barracks and the royal stables are situated here. The city is also notable as having been the starting point for Ramses' great battle in Kadesh in the fifth year of his reign (60 years ago). The stables, should you get the

Many mansions boast a sunken limestone bath.

opportunity to visit, are immense and hold as many as 500 of the best horses in Egypt.

As a harbor town Pr-Rameses is also a great place for the visitor to purchase any number of imported items straight off the boat, including oils, perfumes, wood, stone, and metals.

Pr-Rameses is the official residence of Ramses Usermaatra-Setepenra, and his palace can be found in the very heart of the town—although it is not open to the public.

There are also a number of temples in the city: four large ones, each approached by an elaborate sphinx avenue, and a number of smaller shrines and chapels, which are easier to gain access to.

The main temple, which is dedicated to Amun-Re-Horakhty-Atum, is in the center of the city near the palace, and equals Ipet-sut in size. Its main gateway is dominated by four colossal statues, creating a façade similar to that of Abu Simbel (see p. 94). Most of these temples are dedicated to various personal gods of Ramses, although the main cult in the eastern Delta and Pr-Rameses is the god of chaos, Seth—who is the patron deity of the Ramesside family.

WHAT TO EXPECT

THE WORSHIP OF SETH

There are numerous temples to the god Seth at Pr-Rameses, something that you will not see elsewhere in Egypt. Generally people are unnerved by the god of chaos, and feel safer not worshipping him.

For the visitor to Egypt this deity may seem unusual, as he is part-man, part-animal, but the animal part is unrecognizable. The animal represents chaos, an anti-animal. Although the god of chaos, Seth is not evil; he is simply the opposite to the order represented by the god Horus. Without chaos, order cannot exist; without Seth, Horus would be irrelevant.

Throughout Egyptian history the king has been an incarnation of the god Horus, although a handful—including the current king and his father, Sety—while still being the "Living Horus," have adopted the god Seth as their own.

THE CAPITAL OF MENNEFER

IN THE NORTH OF EGYPT IT IS ESSENTIAL TO VISIT THE CITY OF MENNEFER ("ESTABLISHED AND BEAUTIFUL"). THE CAPITAL OF THE FIRST LOWER EGYPTIAN NOME, AND THE ADMINISTRATIVE CAPITAL OF EGYPT, IT HAS RETAINED ITS IMPORTANCE AS A RELIGIOUS AND ADMINISTRATIVE CENTER SINCE THE EARLIEST TIMES. BELIEVED TO HAVE BEEN FOUNDED BY KING MENES, A SUCCESSOR OF NARMER, IT WAS THE ROYAL RESIDENCE DURING ITS EARLIEST DAYS AND WAS KNOWN AS INEB-HEDJ (WHITE WALLS), AFTER ITS FORTIFIED PALACE.

As a royal residence, the royal cemeteries here are immense—covering over 6,603 square cubits. There are only a few burials actually within the city itself, in a small cemetery used for about 130 years after the end of the pyramid age. All the other cemeteries are on the west bank of the Nile.

The location of Mennefer is an important one for the control of traffic from the south and from the Delta; and as it is situated on the Nile it is a prime location for a major harbor. Indeed, all trade from the northern territories comes through here.

This has led to Mennefer's rise as a trading city, with merchants, sailors, and soldiers thronging the streets, and workshops constantly producing goods for export.

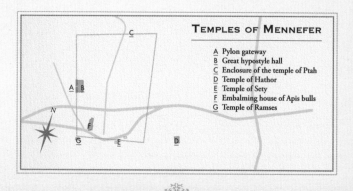

TEMPLES OF MENNEFER

A Pylon gateway
B Great hypostyle hall
C Enclosure of the temple of Ptah
D Temple of Hathor
E Temple of Sety
F Embalming house of Apis bulls
G Temple of Ramses

THE MEMPHITE THEOLOGY

When visiting the sacred city of Mennefer, you will notice that the god Ptah is revered here as the supreme creator.

According to legend, Ptah was present before the primeval mound, and created for himself a physical form before creating the mound upon which the known world was born. Creation came about through a desire in Ptah's heart, which became manifest when he uttered the Word. In this way he pronounced the name of the god Atum, who came into existence as the sun god, who was then responsible for the creation of the next generation of deities, Shu and Tefnut (air and moisture) through the act of masturbation. They in turn gave birth, in the more usual fashion, to Geb and Nut (earth and sky), who also coupled, giving birth to Osiris, Isis, Nephthys, and Seth.

Ptah, in the meantime, created the remainder of the known world, including all the gods, all humankind, all cattle, and all creeping things that live. At Mennefer it is believed that Ptah is present in all living creatures.

Ptah, the supreme creator.

THE CULT OF PTAH

Mennefer is the cult center for Ptah, his consort Sekhmet, and child Nefertum; and the main temple here is for Ptah. There has been a temple here for centuries, although the one standing today is newly built by Ramses. He has reused some of the Saqqara pyramid's casing blocks and also replaced earlier temples of Amenemhat Nymaatra, Thutmosis Menkheperre, and Amenhotep Nebmaatra.

The pylon gateway to the west entrance of the religious enclosure belongs to Ramses, as well as the smaller entrances to the north and the south of the enclosure. These are made more elaborate by his less-than-subtle placement of colossal statues of himself, emphasizing that the deified Ramses is himself worshipped here.

Just outside the walls of the Ptah complex, to the east, Ramses has constructed a small temple dedicated to Hathor; and to the southwest of the Ptah temple lies a statue temple, dedicated to the deified form of himself, firmly stamping his name on Mennefer as the builder of temples.

TEMPLE OF RA AT IUNU

THE CITY OF IUNU HAS BEEN IMPORTANT SINCE THE PYRAMID AGE AND HAS BEEN A MODEL FOR A NUMBER OF MAJOR CITIES SINCE, INCLUDING THEBES ITSELF. IT IS THE CAPITAL OF THE 13TH LOWER EGYPTIAN NOME AND HAS REMAINED AT THE FOREFRONT OF SOLAR WORSHIP; KINGS HAVE BEEN ADDING TO THIS TEMPLE AND INDEED TO THIS GREAT CITY FOR OVER A THOUSAND YEARS. ONE OF THE EARLIEST KINGS ATTESTED HERE IS DJOSER, THE BUILDER OF THE STEP PYRAMID.

Iunu was a particularly important site for the solar and funerary cults, hence a number of the pyramid fields lie in sight of the temple from the west bank of the Nile. Not only were the tombs visible from the temple, but the temple was in sight of the tombs.

To the southeast of Iunu lies the Red Mountain and its quarry for quartzite, from which many features of the Giza, Mennefer, and Iunu monuments are built. This is a particularly difficult stone to quarry and is therefore used for only those statues and inscriptions of the highest quality.

THE MAIN TEMPLE

The main temple at Iunu, known as Hwt Aat (the Great Shrine) was built on a mound known as the "High Sand," in the center of the temple enclosure, which stretches for over 1,886 cubits from east to west. This mound is thought by Egyptians to be the Mound of Creation from which life itself first sprung.

Obelisks are also an adaptation of the *benben* stone, representative of the Mound of Creation, and therefore an appropriate focus of the temple; indeed there are a number erected here. The earliest visible temple on this mound was built just after the end of the Pyramid Age.

The highlights of this project are the two standing obelisks of Senusret Kheperkara flanking the doorway of the great temple in the center of the religious enclosure, although the earliest obelisks at the site were constructed by Tety, one of the later kings of the Pyramid Age, and there may be a structure beneath this one of this earlier date. Thutmosis Menkheperre also added three pairs of obelisks to the site, and the size of these is on a par with those of Ramses at Luxor.

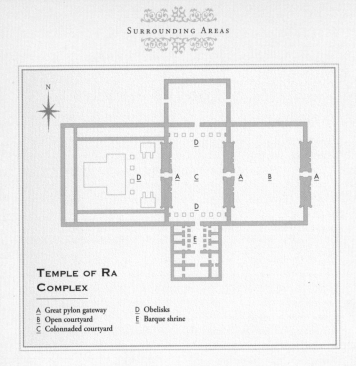

TEMPLE OF RA COMPLEX

A Great pylon gateway
B Open courtyard
C Colonnaded courtyard
D Obelisks
E Barque shrine

In total there are 16 obelisks at the temple, and with this number of obelisks at the site the eye is automatically drawn toward the sky and the sun.

RECENT ADDITIONS

The current king Ramses has also made his contributions at Iunu in the form of colossal statues, and his father Sety erected two limestone pylons complete with obelisks and colossal statues, creating an impressive façade.

The entrance to the main temple is in the east and is reached either by the hilly desert route, or the more scenic waterway, which approaches the temple harbor via the Ity canal before entering the temple along the processional way lined with limestone sphinxes each over 14 cubits in length.

This brings you to two temples: the Atum temple back-to-back with the Ra-Horakhty temple. There are in fact numerous shrines and chapels dedicated by kings in the last 500 years that are attached to the main temple of Ra, and these are growing in number.

As it stands this temple complex is bigger than Ipet-sut (Karnak) in Thebes, and a visitor, if able to gain access, should really dedicate a whole afternoon to the site.

THE SAQQARA COMPLEX

IT WOULD BE A SHAME NOT TO VISIT THE PYRAMIDS THAT EGYPT IS FAMED FOR WHILE YOU ARE IN THE REGION; AND EACH IS A SPECTACULAR MONUMENT OVER 1,200 YEARS OLD. THERE ARE, HOWEVER, OVER A HUNDRED PYRAMIDS IN EGYPT, SO DO NOT EXPECT TO BE ABLE TO VISIT ALL OF THEM—BUT YOU SHOULD TRY TO VISIT THOSE YOU DO SEE IN CHRONOLOGICAL ORDER.

This means that the first stop on your tour should be the step-pyramid complex of Djoser—the first monumental stone structure in the known world—at Saqqara, in the necropolis of Mennefer. The site itself is peppered with pyramid complexes and tombs from the Pyramid Age to the present day.

This pyramid began as a traditional *mastaba* (bench-like) tomb, comprising a burial pit dug into the ground with a bench-shaped mud-brick superstructure

A forerunner of the later pyramids: Djoser's Step Pyramid.

over the top. Initially these were simple mounds of desert rubble, but they gradually became more elaborate, with internal passages and chambers although maintaining the subterranean burial chamber. Initially Djoser had a mastaba of over 130 cubits long and 20 cubits high, but he decided to improve this by extending upwards, adding more bench-like constructions until the six steps were formed that are still visible today.

Each of the stone blocks used to build this structure is of the same size and dimensions as a traditional mud brick, and is designed to last for eternity. It rises over 120 cubits high, and when finished was encased in limestone blocks, giving a smooth, shining finish.

Like all pyramids, the Step Pyramid is part of a wider complex, although this itself differs greatly from others. Djoser constructed a full-sized kingdom that he could rule in the afterlife. However, each of the buildings is a "fake,"

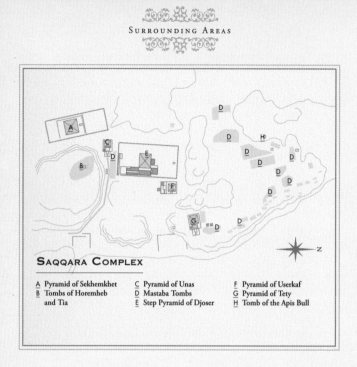

SAQQARA COMPLEX

A Pyramid of Sekhemkhet
B Tombs of Horemheb
and Tia
C Pyramid of Unas
D Mastaba Tombs
E Step Pyramid of Djoser
F Pyramid of Userkaf
G Pyramid of Tety
H Tomb of the Apis Bull

with the doors permanently open, unable to swing shut on stone sockets; rooms and corridors lead to brick walls, and staircases go nowhere. However, it is common knowledge that in the afterlife this site magically becomes "real," providing the king with everything he needs.

There are numerous elements of this complex that are interesting to the visitor, starting with a pillared hall leading to the main complex, where each pillar represents a bundle of reeds. Each pillar is carved out of the walls rather than standing free, thereby creating a series of small chambers. This hall leads to an open court with the markers for the *hebsed* run—in which the king runs around the markers to prove his worth as king. Although this is not in use anymore athletic tourists could try their agility at running these markers in the baking desert heat.

OTHER SITES OF INTEREST

Once the visitor has investigated the dummy buildings of the Djoser complex, he or she can travel to some of the other structures and monuments at Saqqara.

Although the Djoser complex is no longer in use, other features of the area are still being used, and in fact Tia—the sister of Ramses, the current king—has her funerary monument and tomb built here. The temple tomb of the great king

Horemheb is just next to Tia's, and Ramses has in fact added to his sepulcher, in gratitude for his naming of the first Ramses, the king's grandfather, as his successor.

Although it is closed to the public, it is possible to leave offerings for the deceased king's ka at the entrance pylon.

THE TOMB OF THE APIS BULL

To the northwest of the Step Pyramid of Djoser is the tomb of the Apis Bull, a large subterranean structure consisting of large burial chambers for the sacred bulls and their mothers.

The Apis Bull when alive houses the spirit of the god Ptah, and is worshipped locally; however, after death the Apis Bull becomes associated with the god Osiris, while the mother of the bull is upon death associated with Isis.

Although the catacombs are closed to the public, it is possible to leave an offering or a votive stela at the tomb, and there are indeed many of these colorful objects on display.

THE MASTABA TOMBS OF THE PYRAMID AGE

Mastaba tombs were used for both royal and non-royal tombs from the time of Narmer, although they were abandoned by the royals during the Pyramid Age.

The early mastabas comprise a subterranean burial pit with the mud-brick structure over the top, although these slowly developed into more elaborate subterranean structures, with chambers separated by brick partitions. On the whole they are undecorated, but there are a few with elaborately painted burial chambers. As the burials were carried out before the superstructure was built on top, the earlier structures are not accessible to the tourist, although those which have been exposed may be entered.

Later mastabas were, however, completed before burial, and the superstructure is hollow, with a staircase or ramp leading to the burial chambers below ground. These ramps were blocked after burial in an attempt to prevent robbers from infiltrating the tomb and stealing the burial goods. The superstructures function as chapels, where the family can come and leave offerings and prayers to the deceased without entering the burial chamber itself. These often comprise intricate labyrinths of highly decorated rooms.

INSIDE THE TOMBS

Although not officially open to the public, it is possible to enter some of the structures—those with no surviving relatives to maintain the tomb, or those where the families are willing to allow access. There are cemeteries of hundreds of mastaba tombs at many of the pyramid fields in Egypt, occupied by the favored nobles of the pyramid owner. However, some of the most beautiful are those at Giza, Saqqara, and Abdju—so there will always be some nearby to visit.

Once you have gained access to a mastaba, you will be greeted by numerous beautifully carved or painted reliefs of the everyday life of the tomb owner, including scenes of fishing and fowling, hunting, and rather lifelike images of fishermen and butchers at their work. Should you be able to read hieroglyphs, the conversations written above their heads may make you blush—especially those of the fishermen and other boat workers. Meanwhile, the more refined visitor can marvel over the scenes of the jewelry makers, perfume makers, and stonemasons, and then investigate the work in the round in the form of statues in the serdabs, or the ka statues throughout the tombs.

Even those unable to gain access to the tombs should wander in what appears to be a city of the dead. It is a most uplifting experience, with only the wind and the occasional jackal for company.

MERERUKA

Mereruka was the vizier, chief justice, and inspector of the priests and tenants, as well as overseer of the harem during the reign of Tety, some 1,200 years ago. Although he was of noble birth he held his important titles primarily due to his marriage to Seshseshat, the daughter of the king.

His mastaba tomb at Saqqara is within sight of the pyramid of Tety, and is the largest tomb in the cemetery. It has 32 rooms divided into two suites, one for himself and one for his wife. One of his sons, Meri-Tety, was also buried here. The walls of each of these rooms shows very elaborately carved scenes of daily life, including farming, fishing, and the craft workshops that he oversaw in the line of duty. One particularly interesting scene in the suite of Seshseshat actually shows the princess seated on her bed, enticing Mereruka to her with her beautiful harp playing.

Throughout the tomb there are numerous statues of Mereruka, including one emerging from the wall in the pillared hall, as well as numerous life-size statues hidden away in serdabs. There are also numerous false doors carved into the many chambers for offerings of food to be left by the priests or visitors—so come prepared.

THE GREAT PYRAMID OF KHUFU

THE LARGEST PYRAMID ON THE GIZA PLATEAU IS KNOWN LOCALLY AS "AKHET KHUFU"—HORIZON OF KHUFU. IT IS THE LARGEST PYRAMID IN EGYPT, AND IS A SCALED-UP VERSION OF THAT OF SNEFERU, KHUFU'S FATHER, THAT IS FOUND AT DASHUR.

The complex of Khufu consists of the main pyramid itself and three satellite pyramids to the east of the main structure that belong to his queens. The northern satellite pyramid was for his mother Hetepheres, the central one to his wife Meritetes, and the southernmost belonged to Henutsen, his half-sister.

All of these pyramids are within a funerary enclosure consisting of a valley and a mortuary temple joined by a long covered causeway, used for the procession of the mummy from one temple to the other prior to burial. There is also a large cemetery of mastaba tombs for his family and other nobles.

KHUFU'S PYRAMID

Khufu's pyramid stands 275 cubits high and is encased in polished limestone blocks. Some of these blocks are, however, sadly being removed for modern building

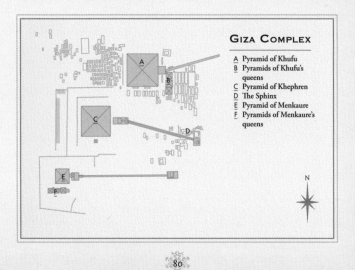

GIZA COMPLEX

A Pyramid of Khufu
B Pyramids of Khufu's
   queens
C Pyramid of Khephren
D The Sphinx
E Pyramid of Menkaure
F Pyramids of Menkaure's
   queens

N

works in the area. It is unlikely that the pyramid will be accessible to the tourist, but it is rumored to have a very complex internal structure with a long descending passage leading to two or three subterranean chambers, with extra corridors leading to the burial chamber of the king.

The complex at Giza consists of more than just the Great Pyramid.

Due to the size of the monument, the internal structure needs to support a great weight, probably in the same way as the Dashur pyramid which has a central corridor with a corbeled roof. Above the burial chamber, in the center of the structure rather than underground, there are probably weight-supporting chambers preventing the roof from collapsing under the pressure.

As it is not possible to enter the pyramids, the visitor needs to concentrate on the surrounding area. Just to the side of Khufu's pyramid are five full-size boat pits, sealed with huge slabs of limestone, and presumably there are full-size boats in each. The funeral of the king included at least one wooden barge bringing the mummy from

---

WHAT TO EXPECT

What Does it Take to Build a Pyramid?

When you arrive at the Great Pyramid of Khufu the first thing that will strike you is its size. Each block is nearly the height of a man, each dragged into place by a team of strong workmen. Once they have recovered from the shock of the scale, many speculate as to how many blocks were used to construct it. Many a night has been spent debating this question, with estimations between 700,000 and nearly 4,000,000. But no one will ever know the answer without dismantling the pyramid!

The whole structure is encased in beautiful white limestone from the quarry at Tura, near Giza.

the east to the west bank, so at least one of these pits contains this funerary boat. The dimensions and material of the boat have been lost over the centuries, but it was not uncommon for such vessels to be dismantled for burial.

Once the visitor has marveled at the size and structure of the pyramids at the site, the next logical place to visit would be the mastaba tombs of the Pyramid Age—namely the necropolis of the nobles of Khufu, Khafra, and Menkaure.

HOW THE PYRAMIDS WERE BUILT

The question that goes through the mind of all visitors as they stand before a monument such as Khufu's pyramid is "how were they built?" Well, for a start up to 20,000 people were hired to build the pyramid of Khufu.

The first stage was to level the ground before the corners of the pyramid were oriented to the four cardinal points by lining them up with the northern star. Once these preliminaries had been completed, the building proper commenced.

The blocks were dragged from the quarries, with men placing logs before each block to create a system of rollers. As the structure grew the methods changed. The maneuvering of the blocks onto the second layer and above, was facilitated by levers and rockers each handled by a team of four.

As the pyramid got higher construction ramps were used: for the smaller pyramids a single ramp projected from one side, but for the larger ones a spiraling ramp was employed. For the pyramid of Khufu these ramps would be inappropriate due to the sheer size, so four staircases were used—one on each side of the pyramid.

Once the entire pyramid had been built, the limestone casing blocks were slipped into place, before being smoothed and polished. The most important part of the pyramid was the benben stone, or pyramid-shaped mound of stone placed at the summit. Some of these stones were gilded in either gold or electrum, although even with the Medjay patrolling, this gold has quickly been stripped and melted down.

THE SPHINX

One of the most striking aspects of the Giza Plateau is the colossal sphinx, the first monument of its kind in Egypt. It is situated at the end of the causeway leading to Khufu's pyramid.

It took some 20,000 men to build Khufu's Great Pyramid.

*The Sphinx of Khafra guards
the Giza Plateau.*

The sphinx displays the reddish-brown face of King Khafra, wearing the blue and gold nemes headdress, and false beard, all atop the body of a lion. His role is primarily to guard the plateau, although the sphinx is a deity in his own right; the solar god Horemakhet (Horus in the Horizon). This deity is closely connected with the king and his divine power and the lion represents a solar symbol and the might and strength of the king. A newly carved colossal statue now stands under the chin of the sphinx showing the god protecting the king; reasserting this connection.

The sphinx and nearby sphinx temple dedicated to the king and Horemakhet were completed by Khafra, but since then each king has made additions and improvements. The most prominent addition is the open-air chapel between the feet of the sphinx. In order to gain the approval and support of the solar deity, Thutmosis cleared the sand away from the monument and made repairs to the temenos wall. Embedded within this new mud-brick wall are 17 carved stelae dedicated by Thutmosis to the Sphinx, as well as a number of small stela dedicated by rich officials. As they are over 300 years old they are worth making the effort to see, if only for the colorful inscriptions and images.

Larger additions than this have also been made, including a way station, for refreshing the gods during processions, built by Amenhotep Aakheperure, and even a royal hunting lodge from the time before Horemheb. This lodge was used by the royal party whilst hunting in the desert and visiting the temples of the sphinx. There are two colossal statues, built by Thutmosis Menkheperure standing upon stone plinths on the north and south of the sphinx body dedicated to Osiris which are ideal places to leave offerings of food and prayers. Although primarily a place of royal pilgrimage the visitor should not be discouraged from leaving their own votive offerings. Anyone can leave such an offering and the inscriptions show the names and titles of soldiers, officials and even lowly goatherds.

KHEMENU (HERMOPOLIS)

THE TOWN OF HERMOPOLIS, KNOWN LOCALLY AS KHEMENU ("THE EIGHT") IS SITUATED IN MIDDLE EGYPT ON THE WEST BANK OF THE NILE, AND IS NAMED AFTER THE EIGHT DEITIES LINKED TO THE OGDOAD MYTH OF CREATION. THE CITY WAS THE CAPITAL OF THE 15TH UPPER EGYPTIAN NOME AND IS DEDICATED TO THE GOD OF WISDOM AND HEALING, THOTH (INSET). THE SITE HAS A LONG HISTORY, BUT IT IS ONLY REALLY IN THE LAST 500 YEARS OR SO THAT NEW CONSTRUCTION HAS BEGUN HERE.

The main religious center is enclosed within a large walled area. Some of the earliest remains from the site are from the reign of Amenemhat Nubkaure, who built a small shrine to Djehuty and the primordial gods; followers of this cult believe this temple was built on the original primeval Mound of Creation.

In the eastern area is a smaller secondary enclosure with another shrine dedicated to Djehuty, and to the west is the east–west oriented chapel of Amun, built by the current king, Ramses. In fact this whole enclosure is entered via the monumental pylon gateway constructed by him, approached by a processional way. The small

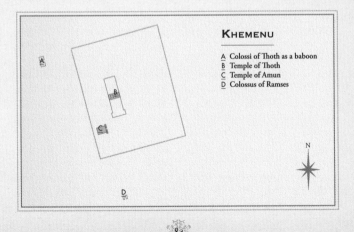

KHEMENU

A Colossi of Thoth as a baboon
B Temple of Thoth
C Temple of Amun
D Colossus of Ramses

N

shrine to Amun is in the style of a "House of Millions of Years" or mortuary temple, and has a turreted fortress wall and a cult palace. To the south of the enclosure Ramses has also constructed a small shrine to the god Ptah, the creator deity of Mennefer, and the god of craftsmen.

To the north of the entrance to the small enclosure is the main temple of the site, oriented north to south, entered via a further pylon and a pillared hallway. Within the temple are four colossal quartzite statues of Djehuty in baboon form dedicated by the great Amenhotep Nebmaatra. This statue is the focus of the temple, and is the site of many pilgrimages to ask for help from the god of healing.

The officials who resided in Khemenu 700 years ago were buried in the nearby necropolis of el Bersha, which comprises some of the most beautifully decorated rock-cut tombs, very similar to those at Beni Hasan. The Coffin Texts of this area are particularly impressive, as would be expected of those who have dedicated their lives to the god of knowledge and the inventor of hieroglyphs, Djehuty.

The Khnum of Khemenu (Ogdoad of Hermopolis)

The city of Khemenu received its name from the creation myth of the Ogdoad of Khemenu. These were the eight deities present before the Mound of Creation emerged from the primeval waters. There were four frogs (male) and four snakes (female) that mated within the primeval waters, their movements causing the dynamics which pushed the mound out of the water upon which all creation began. Each of these couples represents a concept: Nun (male) and Naunet (female) represent water; Amun (male) and Amunet (female) represent hiddenness; Heh (male) and Hauhet (female) represent infinity; while Kek (male) and Kauket (female) represent darkness.

Once the Mound of Creation had emerged from the primeval water, the *benu* bird (phoenix) laid the cosmic egg from which the sun rose for the first time. This sunrise saw the "birth" of Atum and the start of the Heliopolitan myth from Iunu.

BENI HASAN

THIS SITE ON THE EAST BANK OF THE NILE IN MIDDLE EGYPT IS THE NECROPOLIS FOR THE MAYORS OF THE ORYX NOME (16TH UPPER EGYPTIAN NOME), AT ITS PEAK BETWEEN 900 AND 700 YEARS AGO. THERE ARE 39 ROCK-CUT TOMBS HERE ON A HIGH RIDGE IN THE CLIFFS.

To reach the site it is more enjoyable to arrive by boat and arrange for donkeys to take you up the cliff face—although some of it may need to be traversed on foot. Although this is a difficult site to get to, it is well worth the effort, as the views of the Nile from the ridge are stunning, and there are some lovely chapels where a visitor can sit in the shade, and have lunch.

The decoration within these tomb chapels is very informative of life in this region and the role carried out by the local mayors. Many of the chapels themselves are open, if not to the public then to the descendants who may attend the chapels to leave offerings to the spirits of the deceased. The burial chambers are under the chapels at the end of long shafts.

INSIDE THE TOMBS

The general layout of all the tombs starts with a forecourt in front of the tomb, with a pillared façade occasionally decorated with carved and painted relief. The tomb entrance leads the visitor into the cliff face and a large pillared hall, reminiscent of a domestic interior, but highly decorated with painted relief. At the rear of the hall is a small statue shrine containing a ka statue of the tomb owner—at whose feet offerings of food and goods can be left.

It will be sheer luck as to which tombs you gain access to, but all have beautiful decoration. In the tomb of Khnumhotep look for the image of the farmers picking figs and placing them in a large basket—the baboon in the tree is helping himself to fruit and generally causing the farmers problems. The tomb of Baqet has some lovely scenes of weaving, spinning, goldsmiths, and sculptors. The tomb of Khety displays some very dynamic images of soldiers in training including wrestling, weightlifting, and stick fighting.

Many of the tombs have the famous fishing and fowling scenes that show the tomb owner in the marshes hunting birds

The scenes of fishing and fowling that decorate many tomb interiors.

and catching fish. The tomb of Khnumhotep also boasts an image of a trading expedition between the local governor and the Heqa Haswt, the Asiatics, who gained control over Egypt until the great Ahmose expelled them—a most unusual representation.

THE SPEOS ARTEMIDOS

Just to the south of the Beni Hasan necropolis is the rock-cut shrine of Sety Menmaatra, called the Speos Artemidos which consists of a vestibule and a shrine joined by a short corridor.

Sety was not the original builder of the shrine, as he usurped it, although Thutmosis Menkheperre had already added his name to the original inscriptions.

This shrine was dedicated to the local lion-headed goddess Pakhet ("She who Scratches"), but is unfinished. There are roughly cut Hathor-headed columns in the

entrance façade, and unfinished Osiride columns at the rear. A sanctuary at the rear of the temple has a statue of the goddess Pakhet.

One interesting text describes some of the destruction caused by the Heqa Haswt and the repairs carried out by the builder of the temple. Although an important text this is pure propaganda as the temple was built a century or so after the Heqa Haswt were expelled from Egypt.

The Speos Artemidos shrine south of the Beni Hasan necropolis.

ABDJU

THE SITE OF ABDJU, JUST NORTH OF THEBES, HAS BEEN IMPORTANT FOR THOUSANDS OF YEARS. THE KINGS OF THE EARLIEST PERIOD ARE ALL BURIED HERE, AND THE FATHER OF THE CURRENT KING BUILT HIS MORTUARY TEMPLE HERE, WHICH HAS BEEN COMPLETED AND IMPROVED BY RAMSES. THE SITE BOASTS CONNECTIONS WITH THE GOD OSIRIS.

In the Osiris and Seth mythology, when Osiris was dismembered and his body scattered throughout Egypt, it is said that his head was dropped at Abdju. However, it is more commonly believed to be the burial site of the god himself, and all kings wish to be buried in the same place.

Most royal burials do not in fact take place here, but dummy tombs symbolic of burial and royal monuments mean that a king's ka can travel here in the afterlife.

Ahmose, the king who forced the Heqa Haswt rulers from Egypt, built a funerary complex here. This consists of a pyramid-like construction, a chapel dedicated to his grandmother Tetisheri, a terraced temple, and an unfinished tomb to Osiris.

THE TEMPLE OF SETY MENMAATRA

The main building at the site is the mortuary temple of Sety Menmaatra, the father of the

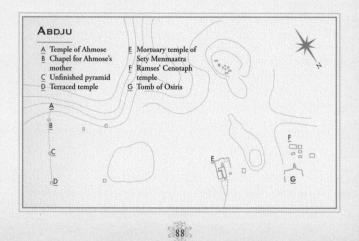

ABDJU

A Temple of Ahmose
B Chapel for Ahmose's mother
C Unfinished pyramid
D Terraced temple
E Mortuary temple of Sety Menmaatra
F Ramses' Cenotaph temple
G Tomb of Osiris

current king, who has expanded it. This is a complex temple with some of the most stunning raised-relief decoration in Egypt. One architectural element of the Sety temple is the seven chapels leading off the main hypostyle hall, each decorated with colorful illustrations of the festivals that were carried out within. One of the most spectacular scenes is of the young prince Ramses (before he came to the throne) participating in his first wild-bull hunt, aided by his father. This was the time that king Sety realized his son was suitable to ascend to the throne.

Ramses himself has built a cenotaph temple at the site, to the northwest of his father's temple.

The temple of Sety at Abdju boasts the finest raised relief in Egypt.

Although on a smaller scale, it is a copy of his mortuary temple at Thebes, consisting of a pylon and colonnaded courtyard, leading to two chapels at the rear of the temple, one dedicated to the deified Sety, and the other to the Ennead of the creation myths.

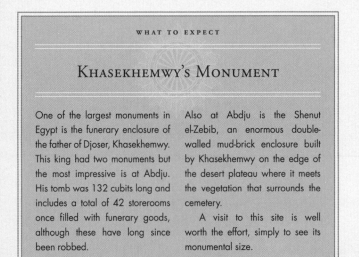

WHAT TO EXPECT

KHASEKHEMWY'S MONUMENT

One of the largest monuments in Egypt is the funerary enclosure of the father of Djoser, Khasekhemwy. This king had two monuments but the most impressive is at Abdju. His tomb was 132 cubits long and includes a total of 42 storerooms once filled with funerary goods, although these have long since been robbed.

Also at Abdju is the Shenut el-Zebib, an enormous double-walled mud-brick enclosure built by Khasekhemwy on the edge of the desert plateau where it meets the vegetation that surrounds the cemetery.

A visit to this site is well worth the effort, simply to see its monumental size.

KEBET (COPTOS)

THE CITY OF KEBET IS AN IMPORTANT ONE TO THE WHOLE OF EGYPT, AND AS SUCH IT IS WELL WORTH A VISIT. AS THE CAPITAL OF THE FIFTH UPPER EGYPTIAN NOME IT LIES SOME 7,547 CUBITS NORTH OF THEBES, AT THE ENTRANCE TO THE WADI HAMMAMAT ON THE EAST BANK OF THE NILE, AND IS THE STARTING POINT FOR EXPEDITIONS TO THE GOLD MINES AND BRECCIA QUARRIES NEARBY IN THE EASTERN DESERT. IT IS ALSO ON THE ROUTE TO THE RED SEA; SO, AS THE VISITOR MAY WELL IMAGINE, IT IS A VERY BUSY CITY, WITH TRADERS, SOLDIERS, AND SHOPPERS MILLING AROUND—AND ITS LONG HISTORY MEANS THAT IT HAS BEEN THIS WAY FOR OVER 2,000 YEARS.

One of the most unusual sights will be soldiers dismantling boats to be carried over the eastern desert to the Red Sea, where they are rebuilt and then used on trading or military expeditions. If you are lucky you will see the expeditions making headway in long regimented lines with donkeys laden with goods to exchange. This city is therefore a good place to pick up exotic goods before they appear on the open market.

THE CULT OF MIN

In addition to being an ancient town Kebet is also a major cult center for the deity Min, a fertility god often associated with the god Amun at Karnak. At Kebet there are at least three new temples, although their site has been in use for thousands of years.

Evidence of early worship can be seen in the three colossal statues of Min, each 9 cubits high and believed to be the earliest colossal statues in Egypt, dating to over 2,300 years ago. At that time Kebet was a large town, and there is a large cemetery to the east of the modern settlement, although there are no visible funerary superstructures to mark the graves.

The temples currently on the site are of newer construction, and are surrounded by a thick enclosure wall. The main temple to Min was initially built at the end of the Pyramid Age, by Senusret Kheperkara, but was rebuilt by Thutmosis Menkheperre—his monumental gateway is still used to enter the structure.

Thutmosis also built a smaller temple to Min and Isis, again by

MIN

The god Min, "He of the Eastern Desert," is worshipped at the site of Kebet and has been for nearly 2,500 years.

Min is shown in mummiform, with his right armed raised and his left arm holding his erect phallus as a sign of his fertility. Sometimes his skin is shown painted black—a reflection of the fertility of the black Nile silt. He is a very old deity, but in the last few centuries he has become more closely associated with Horus and Amun.

Min is often depicted alongside his sacred lettuce, the fetish closely associated with him. The lettuce is seen to have aphrodisiacal properties and the liquid that comes from the stem is often associated with fertility.

At the start of the harvest season the small statue of Min from within the temple shrines is taken in procession to the fields, where he cast his favor over them, thereby ensuring that a good harvest will follow.

The statue of the fertility god Min—the oldest colossal statue in Egypt.

dismantling the earlier temple of Amenemhat Sehetepibre and Senusret Kheperkara. Although nothing of the earlier temples remains, it is common knowledge that the site itself has been in constant use since even before the time of Narmer.

MEDAMUD

WHILST IN THE THEBAN REGION, IF YOU FANCY SOMETHING A LITTLE OFF THE BEATEN TRACK WHY NOT VISIT THE ANCIENT TEMPLE OF MEDAMUD (KNOWN LOCALLY AS MADU), SITUATED 9,433 CUBITS NORTHEAST OF KARNAK TEMPLE?

There has been a temple on this site from the Pyramid Age dedicated to the lunar deity Montu, the god of war. The site consists of two mounds, upon which the original temple was built. This temple was very unusual (see opposite), and some think it is a shame that it was knocked down, even though the temple that replaced it is far more beautiful.

This earlier structure was replaced by Senusret Khakhaure. It is now a small construction made of mud brick. The columns and the pylons, however, are built of solid stone, giving the approach to the temple an appearance of splendor. Every king since Thutmosis has made additions to the temple and it has remained popular amongst the kings as a place of worship.

There is also an enclosure wall surrounding a number of priests' houses, grain silos, and a small cult temple with royal statue pillars. This may be the only place that tourists will have access to, and is therefore a good place to start as the priests may be persuaded to allow a visitor to enter the main enclosure.

Montu, the Egyptian god of war, for whom the temple of Medamud is dedicated.

THE PYRAMID-AGE TEMPLE OF MEDAMUD

The Pyramid-Age temple at Medamud is different from any other temple in Egypt.

The temple is enclosed within a trapezoidal wall. This enclosure was entered by the first of two brick pylons. The temple within the enclosure wall consists of a courtyard between the first and second pylons, the second leading to the rear of the temple.

It is in this area that the temple becomes unusual. Outside the walls of this temple are two mounds, and atop each was a small enclosure, surrounded by a lush garden of trees. Subterranean chambers within the mounds were reached by two corridors (one to each structure) starting at the rear of the main temple.

Who this temple was dedicated to has long been forgotten, especially as the site is now dedicated to the god Montu. The mounds are thought to represent the Mound of Creation, and the trees show the fertility of the site. Some have suggested that the temple may also have been dedicated to an early form of Hathor, the Lady of the Sycamore, and the trees could represent the nurturing of this goddess.

The impressive lintel of Senusret gives the temple of Medamud a breathtaking entranceway.

NUBIA

THE BOUNDARIES OF NUBIA HAVE SLOWLY CHANGED OVER
THE CENTURIES, EXTENDING FURTHER SOUTH, ALTHOUGH
THE OFFICIAL BOUNDARY IS AT ELEPHANTINE. HOWEVER,
DURING THE REIGN OF RAMSES THERE IS A GREAT EGYPTIAN
PRESENCE—AND NUMEROUS STRUCTURES BUILT BY THE KING
HIMSELF—BEYOND ELEPHANTINE.

ASWAN

For the visitor who wants to get
away from the hustle and bustle
of the metropolis of Thebes, why
not travel southwards to Aswan,
just south of the Egyptian border?
A slow cruise down the Nile is
the most relaxing way to arrive,
and affords you the opportunity
to see the beautiful scenery and
arrive refreshed and relaxed. Bear
in mind, though, that the further
south you go the hotter it is.

There is plenty to see in the
region, although some temples
are more impressive than others.
When you first arrive, why not go
for a walk through the cemetery
with tombs from the Pyramid Age
onwards? The older tomb of Sabni
and Mehu is reached via a staircase
directly from the river bank. As
you reach the entrance there is
a beautiful obelisk-shaped stela,
which is worth seeing even if you
are unable to enter the sepulcher.

The thousand-year-old tombs
of Sarenput and Heqaib are
also reached by a staircase from

the Nile, but these have a large
courtyard cut into the cliffs with a
portico at the rear before you reach
the tomb entrance itself.

Within the tombs, if you can
gain access, you may see some very
elaborate mummiform statues in
the chapel area carved directly
from the rock where the light was
channelled in. It is a very serene
and atmospheric ambience.

THE TEMPLES AT ABU SIMBEL

The amazing temples at Abu
Simbel, built by the current king
of Egypt, are only two of seven
rock-cut temples built by him in
the area, but are by far the most
impressive. The monuments at
Abu Simbel took the king 30 years
to complete, being dedicated to the
gods in year 35 of his reign—some
30 years ago.

There are two temples on the
site: one dedicated to Re-Horakhty,
Ptah, Amun-Re, and Ramses
himself, known locally as "The
Temple of Ramses, Beloved of

*Four colossal statues of Ramses guard the entrance
to his temple at Abu Simbel.*

of Amun;" and the other dedicated to the king's first Great Royal Wife, Nefertari, who died just prior to the temple being dedicated to the goddess Hathor.

When you arrive at the site, approach the larger of the two temples, dedicated to the deified Ramses. The façade of this temple can be seen long before it is reached, and looming from the living rock are four colossal seated statues of the king, each standing 39 cubits high. Around the feet and legs of the king are images of the Great Royal Wife Nefertari and Ramses' mother Tuya, and a number of his daughters.

Before the façade there is a large forecourt approached by a sphinx avenue, with two tanks used by the priests to purify themselves before entering the temple.

On entering the main temple, through the door between the second and third colossal statues, you will find yourself in an imposing pillared hall dominated by eight colossal pillar statues showing Ramses in mummiform holding the crook and flail. Behind these pillars on the walls are polychrome images of the great battle victories of Ramses, including another representation of the battle of Kadesh. As you continue along the central axis of the temple you enter another pillared hall, smaller than the first and decorated with images of the

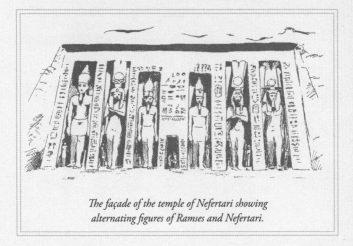

*The façade of the temple of Nefertari showing
alternating figures of Ramses and Nefertari.*

king making offerings to the gods. At the rear of the temple, deep in the cliff side, there is a small sanctuary filled with four rock-cut statues of the deities to whom the temple is dedicated. Small rooms off this chamber are for the storage of the cult objects and will be strictly off-limits to tourists.

If time permits, once leaving this temple walk northwards to the small temple of Hathor and

SUNRISE AT ABU SIMBEL

The main temple of Ramses faces east so the rising sun shines on the façade of the temple. There is a frieze of baboons at the top of the façade, representing the solar baboons who greet the sun daily. Twice a year, in the second month of Akhet and the second month of Proyet, the sun shines through the door straight down the central axis onto the four statues in the sanctuary at the back, emphasizing the solar aspects of the temple cult. The statues are painted in vivid colors, and show the king as a divine being.

Nefertari. You will be greeted by the rock-cut facade with six standing colossal statues each 18 cubits high, two of Nefertari and three of Ramses. Within the temple there is only one pillared hall, with beautiful painted Hathor-headed columns. The next chamber along the central axis is small and decorated with images of both the king and queen interacting with the gods. In the sanctuary at the rear of the temple is a spectacular image of the goddess Hathor, as a cow emerging from the living rock; a fitting focus to the cult of the temple.

GERF HUSSAIN

While traveling in the Nubian region, why not visit the small, newly built temple at Gerf Hussain (known locally as "The Temple of Ramses-Meryamun in the Domain of Ptah"), built by the current king, Ramses Usermaatra-Setepenra in year 35 of his reign? It is situated on the west bank of the Nile and is dedicated to Ptah, Ptah-Tanen, Hathor, and the divine Ramses himself. There are statues of these deities carved directly from the living rock at the back of the temple in the sanctuary. This temple is built in two parts: one free-standing and the other carved directly into the cliff, the building of which was supervised by the Viceroy of Kush, Setau.

You approach the temple by river, and there is a ceremonial avenue of ram-headed sphinxes leading to the first, free-standing pylon. The forecourt of the temple, open to the sun as is traditional in temples of this period, has eight stocky colossal statue-pillars of the king and six ordinary pillars. Ramses adopted the blocky Nubian artistic style rather than the slender form used in Egypt.

The rear aspect of the temple is cut from the rock face and resembles Abu Simbel, with a pillared hall, and four statue niches housing statues of the divine triad, and in the rear is a barque shrine with an offering table and statues of the main deities of the temple. If you can gain access to this part of the temple you will find these statues glittering in the lamplight, as they are all gilded with the gold abundant in the area. The statue of Ptah-Tanen even has a beautifully carved hawk above his head.

The impressive entrance of Ramses' temple at Gerf Hussain.

ENTERTAINMENT
ON A BUDGET

*There are many ways to pass the time in Egypt, and the
Egyptians are a fun-loving people. The variety of
sporting and cultural pursuits that are on offer will
give you a great insight into Egyptian society, whether
you are just relaxing in a public square and engaging
one of the locals in a game of "Dogs and Jackals," or
taking in the thrilling spectacle of Egypt's most popular
sport, wrestling.*

FESTIVALS

NO VISITOR TO EGYPT CAN FAIL TO SEE HOW MUCH THE
EGYPTIANS LOVE FESTIVALS. THEY ARE USED TO WORSHIP
THE GODS, TO DINE WITH FRIENDS AND FAMILY, AND TO
ENJOY SOME WELL-EARNED TIME OFF WORK. IN THE THEBAN
REGION, WITH AS MANY AS TWO FESTIVALS OR RELIGIOUS
PROCESSIONS A WEEK, EVEN THE BRIEFEST OF VISITS SHOULD
BE ABLE TO TAKE IN AT LEAST ONE.

A number of festivals and religious practices are the same throughout Egypt, including a procession of the statue of the god in question through the streets, carried in a sacred barque accompanied by priests, priestesses, singers, and dancers, enabling the general populace to address the god with their dilemmas.

This may be followed by offerings to the gods, either through the temple or in household shrines—making some festivals intensely personal affairs. The offerings given to the temples are then distributed to the people, creating an atmosphere of great frivolity. Some festivals last just a day, others for weeks. As soon as you arrive in Thebes, approach the local temple personnel for information on the festivals in the area at that time.

THEBAN FESTIVALS

Festivals specific to the Theban region include the "Beautiful Festival of the Valley" held in the tenth month of the year, which has been carried out for over 500 years. Although a funerary festival, it is one well worth seeing, and is a chance for everyone to remember their ancestors.

This festival starts at the temple of Ipet-sut when the statues of Amun, Mut, and Khonsu are placed within small shrines and loaded onto sacred barques. These are then ferried across the Nile in great splendor, upon a stunning barge.

The sacred barque is carried through the streets during a public festival.

This part of the journey, although short, also includes a great fleet of smaller boats carrying the various participants, and a more beautiful sight is hard to imagine.

Once on the west bank, the procession travels to each mortuary temple in turn, including that of the current king Ramses Usermaatra-Setepenra, and is accompanied by musicians and dancers. The events that take place within these temples are not open to the general public, but if you are lucky you may glimpse the king as he leaves the temple during the journey of the god.

The people of Thebes are encouraged to join in with statues and stelae of their own ancestors, taking them to the funerary chapels in the nearby hills.

For a picturesque view, stand on the east bank at dusk, from where you can see the hundreds of fires dotted amid the cliffs of the west bank, as the locals feast with their ancestors.

WHAT TO EXPECT

FESTIVAL OF DRUNKENNESS

If you travel to Thebes 20 days after the New Year festivals you may be lucky enough to participate in the Festival of Drunkenness, an event in honor of the Golden One, the goddess Hathor.

This festival lasts for five days, and, as the name suggests, involves imbibing excessive amounts of beer and wine. Although some participate for the sheer enjoyment of drinking and dancing with their friends, many people use their inebriated state as a means of communicating with the goddess. The festivities start with an offering to one of the lioness-headed goddesses, Mut or Sekhmet, and the beer drunk—at least initially—is red in reference to the belief that Sekhmet once came close to destroying all of humankind, only to be tricked into drinking beer that was colored red, which she thought was blood.

Once this part is complete, the festivities will move on to the village for more family-oriented celebrations.

WATER SPORTS

THE NILE IS RESPONSIBLE FOR A GREAT DEAL OF THE CHARACTER OF BOTH EGYPT AND EGYPTIANS, AND IS ALSO THE SOURCE OF MUCH PLEASURE. ALL EGYPTIANS SWIM FROM A VERY EARLY AGE, ALTHOUGH THEY HAVE TO BE CAREFUL WHERE THEY DO SO, AS THE NILE IS HOME TO MANY DANGEROUS CREATURES. THERE ARE, HOWEVER, NUMEROUS CANALS AND WATERWAYS FLOWING FROM THE NILE THAT ARE ALMOST ENTIRELY FREE OF DANGER AND ARE AVAILABLE FOR ALL TO SWIM IN.

For the wealthier visitor, a trip to the Fayum for marshland activities is a must. The marshes of the Fayum are teaming with wildlife and are worth visiting just for the views, as well as the opportunity to see various species of fish, fowl, butterflies, grasshoppers, and frogs. The more active holidaymaker can participate in fishing and fowling, both popular pastimes—so popular, in fact, that there is a text in circulation entitled *Pleasures of Fishing and Fowling*. There are numerous ways of doing both activities, depending on your reasons for going.

FISHING

Nets are employed to catch fish in large quantities, either for eating or for selling at market. Two boats sail out together with a net strung between them, while one person

Spearing fish in the Fayum marshes.

An athletic hunter hits his prey with a carefully aimed throwing stick.

in the boat whacks the top of the water with a large stick to attract fish into the net. However, more athletic travelers may want to show off their skills with a spear, by spearing passing fish from atop a flimsy papyrus skiff. If this sounds a little too precarious for your tastes, and you would like a more relaxing break, why not fish with a hook and line, and put your feet up at the edge of the marshes or even by the garden pool of your accommodation. This form of fishing may not yield the same results as net fishing, but it makes for a fun afternoon, and many noblemen take their families on such trips.

FOWLING

Another marshland activity along similar lines is that of fowling—the catching of birds. The more serious fowler catches birds by throwing a large net over the reeds, waiting patiently until they are chased from the bushes by a man yelling at the top of his voice or by cats or dogs. This method will catch hundreds of birds that can be sold at market or eaten at the end of the day. Again, though, there is a more entertaining method that may appeal to the athletic traveler, namely using a throwing stick, which requires a good balance as the stick is thrown from onboard a papyrus skiff. In order to flush out the game, trained cats run into the marshes along the edge of the water, chasing the birds out; as they fly into the air the hunter throws the curved stick as hard as possible, and any birds that are hit are retrieved from where they fall by the cats.

Do not be surprised if the Egyptians leave burnt offerings for Sobek, the crocodile-headed god, before setting off for an afternoon of fishing or fowling. This is simply to ensure that crocodiles will take no notice of the intruders in the marshes. At the end of the trip the Egyptians will offer some of the day's catch to the gods in thanks for their safe return. It won't do you any harm to participate in these rituals.

GENERAL SPORTS

LIKE ALL PEOPLE, EGYPTIANS LOVE COMPETITIVE SPORTS. MOST SPORTS PLAYED ON THE STREETS OF THEBES HAVE THEIR ROOTS IN MILITARY TRAINING. THE MOST POPULAR IS WRESTLING, WHICH HAS BEEN PRACTICED FOR OVER A THOUSAND YEARS. FOR THE LAST FIVE CENTURIES OR SO, WRESTLING HAS ALSO DEVELOPED INTO A DISPLAY SPORT SHOWING OFF THE PARTICIPANTS' STRENGTH, SKILL, AND STAMINA——IT IS OFTEN PART OF MILITARY PRESENTATIONS.

Wrestlers normally compete naked, although a belt is sometimes worn to enable a better grip. Although it may seem tempting, only the stouthearted should consider taking part, as rules are flimsy at best, and a competitor may grab any part of the body to incapacitate his opponent!

Wrestling displays are often accompanied by stick-fighting, another demonstration of skill and strength. In some practice displays the fighters use soft papyrus stalks instead of wooden sticks, whereas soldiers, and often those practicing in the streets, will generally fight with a stick of approximately two cubits in length in either hand, or a single stick in one hand and a protective guard over the wrist of the other.

RUNNING AND JUMPING

Other competitive sports include running and jumping. Running is mostly seen as an endurance sport, and takes place over long distances in extreme heat. Soldiers can often be seen racing each other with a prize and presentation for the winner; however, you may find that you can take part in one of the smaller races held through the streets of the town.

Another particularly popular sport with men is jumping, which is considered to be a display of strength. It is quite simple: each competitor jumps vertically from a standing position, with the one who jumps the highest being declared the winner. Children

Egyptian wrestling is brutal, with no holds barred!

CHARIOT RACING

For the daredevil traveler with an interest in chariot racing, the ancient site of Kom el 'Abd near the city of "Aten is in Splendor," south of Thebes, is worth a visit.

The site may appear barren, but with a little bit of imagination the splendors of the chariot races can be reborn.

The main feature is a straight road that runs until it reaches the base of the cliffs. The road is, however, unpaved and has not been maintained for a century.

To get a good view of the races, observers would ascend a purpose-built ramp cut into the surrounding cliff to a rectangular platform that bears the remains of seven structures that formed the temporary settlement of the caretakers and guards for when the king Amenhotep Nebmaatra came to the site. Why not follow in his footsteps by erecting a tent on the platform and observe the world and the road below from this lofty vantage point?

can often be seen playing the forerunner of this sport in the form of "human hurdles." Two children sit opposite each other with their arms and legs straight, making a hurdle, while another attempts to leap over their arms.

Sport is also incorporated into some religious festivals, and its relation with religion dates at least as far back as the reign of Pepy Neferkara. One such ritual consists of four poles propped against a central pole up which climbers scramble as part of a fertility ritual. A number of men hold ropes tied to the outer poles to steady

Three boys play at "human hurdles."

them, or—if the climber is good enough—to make the task harder by swaying them. Any adults you see climbing trees or poles around the town may be practicing for this ritual, or they may simply be up to no good.

HUNTING

FOR LOCALS AND TOURISTS ALIKE, HUNTING IN EGYPT IS A POPULAR PASTIME. THE DESERTS SURROUNDING THE NILE VALLEY ARE RICH IN LARGE GAME SUCH AS LIONS, LEOPARDS, WILD BULLS, OSTRICHES, ANTELOPES, DEER, AND GAZELLE, ALL SUITED TO THE MORE EXPERIENCED HUNTER. ONCE EGYPTIANS NEEDED TO HUNT FOR FOOD, BUT IN TODAY'S WEALTHY SOCIETY THIS IS NOT NECESSARY, ALTHOUGH WHATEVER IS KILLED STILL BELONGS TO THE HUNTER.

Although many small parties do venture into the desert to hunt, it may be better to try to obtain a place on an organized large-scale hunt, where the animals are "ambushed" by a line of hunters using dogs to flush the prey out. During these hunts it is possible to kill animals in their hundreds, and commemorative records of Thutmosis Menkheperre and Amenhotep Nebmaatra record such vast events.

HUNTING HIPPOS

Hippopotami, which live in abundance in the Nile, are also popular with hunters. However, they are extremely dangerous—especially when protecting their young—and have cost many Egyptians their lives. Hippo hunting has been practiced for over 1,500 years, although originally it was only enjoyed by royalty—both displaying their physical prowess and being symbolic of overcoming evil—but now the upper echelons of society have adopted it more widely as a sport.

Only the brave or foolhardy take on the challenge of hunting hippos.

SKILLS REQUIRED

In order to make the most of hunting in the Theban area, there are various skills in which you must excel, and it is possible to refresh your abilities in relative safety before venturing on a hunt.

Most hunters catch their prey using bow and arrow, and the recently introduced composite bow offers greater accuracy and range than the traditional bow. Various archery competitions offer the chance to improve upon, or even show off, your ability. Although initially intended to showcase the skills of the king, there is nothing to stop non-royals from participating in these tournaments, in which a charioteer, riding at speed, must fire at wooden or copper targets up to three fingers thick.

Particularly talented archers are able to penetrate a target all the way through, or even hit it with more than one arrow at a time. Many kings have boasted that they can fire as many as four arrows at a time! As they are considered divine, this is perhaps not surprising, but few mortals can match their feats.

For hunting large, dangerous animals—such as lions, wild bulls, and even ostriches—it is necessary to use a chariot with a team of two horses and at least two people on the drive plate: one holding the reins, and the other the weapons. High-speed chariot races—either spontaneous or planned—through the desert, are a useful way of getting to know the terrain.

As well as the bow and arrow, some charioteers also feel a spear provides useful protection should a large animal get too close. Prowess with a harpoon is essential for catching and killing a hippo.

Target practice from a fast-moving chariot is a great test of skill.

BOARD GAMES

BOARD GAMES ARE A VERY POPULAR PASTIME IN EGYPT, WITH EVERYONE, INCLUDING THE KING HIMSELF, PLAYING THEM. WHILE TRAVELING THROUGH EGYPT, YOU WILL SEE PEOPLE PLAYING IMPROMPTU GAMES ON MAKESHIFT BOARDS CARVED INTO STONE PAVEMENTS OR DRAWN IN THE SAND, USING SMALL PEBBLES AS THE PIECES. OTHER PEOPLE HAVE ELABORATE BOARDS, EITHER LARGE ONES IN THEIR HOMES OR SMALLER PORTABLE ONES WITH STORAGE SPACE FOR THE PIECES IN THE BASE.

SENET

The most commonly played board game is *senet* the "game of passing," which is played on a board of 30 squares or "houses" in rows of 10. It is a game of strategy and versions of it have been played for over a thousand years. Today each player has five pieces (or "dancers") and the object of the game is to move the pieces over the 30 squares, switching direction at the end of each row until all the pieces have moved off the board.

A senet player about to make his next move.

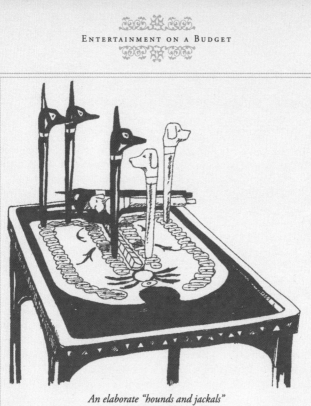

An elaborate "hounds and jackals"
board shown in mid-game.

The number of spaces that a piece must move is determined by throwing four "casting sticks" (wooden sticks with a dark and a light side) and observing the combination that results. Alternatively, one or two sheep knucklebones are used, or even pieces carved in ivory with four faces: flat, concave, convex, and twisted. Each side has a numeric value and the combination thrown determines the move.

In its early years senet was a purely recreational game, but nowadays it has crossed over into the funerary cult as well, and winning a game in the afterlife aids rebirth. Perhaps this is why it is so popular; people feel the need to practice before they die. The game has even been incorporated into chapter 17 of the *Book of The Dead*, and such a scene is also reproduced on a great many papyri and even on the walls of tombs.

MUSIC AND SINGING

NO EGYPTIAN RELIGIOUS OR PUBLIC FESTIVAL, BANQUET OR CELEBRATION, WOULD BE COMPLETE WITHOUT MUSICIANS AND SINGERS. IN FACT, MUSIC AND SONG ARE SO POPULAR THAT THEY ARE INTEGRATED INTO ALL ASPECTS OF LIFE.

For those with monotonous jobs such as crushing grapes at the vineyard, or hauling in fishing nets, a well-known song serves both to maintain a working rhythm and to help pass the time. So don't be surprised by the constant singing from the fields and the workshops. The words to these songs are generally not written down, but if you listen carefully perhaps you can pick out enough to join in—although beware, you may be shocked by the crude lyrics of the fishermen's songs.

Music and singing are so important to the Egyptian people that there are deities associated with them, namely Bes, Ihy, and Hathor; while the god credited with creating both music and song is the god of wisdom, Thoth. This religious connection has ensured that music and song play an important role within temples, and many processions and rituals are accompanied by female musicians shaking the *sistrum* (a sacred rattle) and the *menat* (a beaded necklace) while a songstress sings prayers and hymns in time to the music. These temple musicians are held in high esteem, more so than banquet performers, and are treated with much reverence and respect.

Singers and musicians are available to hire as professional performers for private or public celebrations. Most upper-class banquets will have a troupe of scantily clad women playing lutes, harps, clappers, and flutes, accompanied by drummers or clapping to mark the beat. All the while dancers flit among the guests, swinging their hair from side to side. Some even tie weights into their hair to make it more controllable.

Temple singers practice their art accompanied by a sistrum player.

Large private households may also employ a harpist, quite often blind, to provide entertainment in the evenings, or at low-key dinner parties. Although some noblewomen are able to play instruments, and the walls of the large houses sometimes reverberate with the sounds of the harp or the flute, they never play in public, as it is considered to be socially beneath them.

LOVE SONGS

While wandering the streets of Thebes at night, many a love song can be heard sung by families enjoying some time together, or drunken workmen relaxing after a long day. These love songs vary in style and length: some are sung by men and others by women, some tell of the torments of love, while others offer romantic descriptions of beauty and idealized partners.

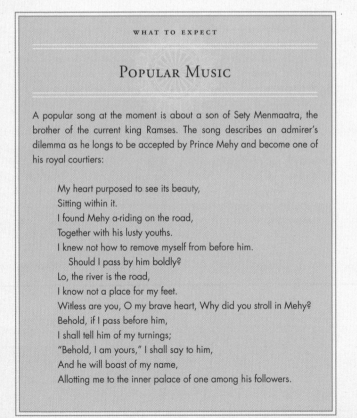

WHAT TO EXPECT

POPULAR MUSIC

A popular song at the moment is about a son of Sety Menmaatra, the brother of the current king Ramses. The song describes an admirer's dilemma as he longs to be accepted by Prince Mehy and become one of his royal courtiers:

My heart purposed to see its beauty,
Sitting within it.
I found Mehy a-riding on the road,
Together with his lusty youths.
I knew not how to remove myself from before him.
   Should I pass by him boldly?
Lo, the river is the road,
I know not a place for my feet.
Witless are you, O my brave heart, Why did you stroll in Mehy?
Behold, if I pass before him,
I shall tell him of my turnings;
"Behold, I am yours," I shall say to him,
And he will boast of my name,
Allotting me to the inner palace of one among his followers.

DANCE

LIKE MUSIC AND SINGING, DANCING IS ALSO POPULAR IN EGYPT. DANCE TROUPES ARE A VERY POPULAR FORM OF ENTERTAINMENT FOR BANQUETS AND PRIVATE EVENTS, AND THEY OFTEN ACCOMPANY A GROUP OF MUSICIANS. THEY ARE GENERALLY PART OF THE SAME TROUPE, WHETHER AS BANQUET OR RELIGIOUS PERFORMERS, AND CAN BE BOOKED AS A COMPLETE PACKAGE.

Some dancers can also play instruments, and it is not unusual for a performer to use a tambourine as part of the routine—keeping her own rhythm. The dancers wear very little, sometimes just a belt and a collar, although some wear diaphanous gowns of high-quality linen, which still leave very little to the imagination. Most dancers are very energetic in their performances, with acrobatics playing an important part in the routine. Don't be shocked to see young naked women doing back-flips, handstands, and cartwheels across the floor; their limited clothing helps retain their agility and flexibility.

Although costume is not so important to professional dancers, their hair is, and it is often used as an integral part of the show. One routine, called the *ib* dance, will appear most bizarre to the newcomer, as the dancers have their hair weighted by balls, and they drag it along the ground to show off their flexibility. Even in more commonplace dances, hair is often used in the routine; whether weighted or not, it is flicked in an erotic manner, first hiding then revealing the face. Because of this it is rare for dancers to wear wigs, but rather they grow their own hair according to modern fashions, and sometimes attach hairpieces

A dance troupe performs at a public gathering.

Muu dancers perform the ritual that
allows a funerary procession to enter the cemetery.

to volumize it, thereby making it more alluring.

Dancers are a vital part of funerary rituals, with a male troupe known as the Muu dancers performing regularly. There are three types of Muu dancers: two have a uniform of tall reed headdresses and kilts, while the third are bare-headed and always dance in pairs. The first group uses specific hand gestures to give permission for a funeral procession to enter the cemetery, while the second guards the cemetery from a high vantage point, and the members of the third group dance in pairs as part a protective ritual.

WHO CAN DANCE?

There are no restrictions on who can become a dancer, although a certain athleticism is necessary. There is no formal training, but like other professions in Egypt there is an apprenticeship scheme,

so a potential trainee needs to find a dancer who will become their mentor and teach them the basics. Some people—dwarfs and pygmies from the south in particular—are actively encouraged to enter into the profession, as they are considered by many Egyptians to be comic—although they are employed in some temple displays as well.

Men and women never dance together. Although both male and female dancers exist, both work in single-sex groups. When dances are performed in pairs they are performed by members of the same sex, and the dancers will mirror each other's movements exactly, displaying the considerable practice and skill that are required of professional performers. But despite this, on your trip to Thebes, why not hire a dancer for an afternoon and try to learn some of the moves?

PUBLIC SQUARES

DUE TO THE HOT CLIMATE THAT PREVAILS IN EGYPT—ESPECIALLY DURING THE SUMMER MONTHS—MANY OF THE DAY-TO-DAY ACTIVITIES TAKE PLACE IN THE OPEN AIR, AS IT IS SIMPLY TOO HOT AND STUFFY INSIDE. ALTHOUGH THE EGYPTIANS ARE RENOWNED AS BEING A VERY SOCIABLE PEOPLE, PUBLIC SQUARES ARE GENERALLY NOT PART OF THE PLAN OF MOST VILLAGES AND TOWNS; HOWEVER, YOU WILL OFTEN FIND THAT AN OPEN SPACE WITHIN THE VILLAGE OR IN THE SURROUNDING AREA HAS BEEN ADOPTED BY THE LOCALS AS A MEETING PLACE.

Even with the existence of these meeting places villagers also meet at local shrines, tombs, and chapels to catch up on the gossip and the local news once they have completed their worship. They may also meet down by the Nile, while bathing, doing the laundry, or fishing.

KEEPING IN TOUCH

But these public spaces are not just useful for people to meet for a chat, they are also valuable areas for conducting business, and it is recommended that any visitor to Thebes locate one of these meeting places. These public areas provide a great place to hear the latest news, often brought by messengers from the king, the military, or other parts of Egypt. Dance troupes and musicians sometimes even put on ad hoc performances here, all for a basic wage as well as to advertise their trade. Local scribes can also be found touting for new work reading or writing letters, witnessing signatures, or writing up legal documents for the locals. Some scribes may set up as teachers in these areas, helping local boys learn the basics of reading and writing in return for a small fee. They may also entertain the local villagers with stories and poetry, both old and new, since written literature is unavailable to many of the people of Egypt.

BUYING AND SELLING

In the absence of an actual marketplace, the public square is put to good use by locals who want to sell their wares, and potential buyers who wish to investigate what is available. Such an area provides space for farmers to bring animals for sale, enabling potential buyers to see them, and a widely known place (especially in Thebes or Memphis) may attract foreign merchants who wish to sell their goods when traveling through the area. Such a public space, even though unofficial, is an important part of the everyday life of most Egyptian villagers. Indeed any traveler who wants to see the "real" Egypt, and perhaps pick up a few souvenirs, or gifts for those at home, really must visit.

WHAT TO EXPECT

FESTIVALS

During festival times some members of the community are given extra food rations by the state to help them to celebrate and to reward them for the work they have done. This extra food is sometimes bestowed in vast quantities; for example, one community was given as much as 150 donkey-loads of provisions, including 9,000 fish, salt for drying, ten oxen ready for slaughter, four donkey-loads of beans and sweet oils, eight donkey-loads of barley malt, 9,000 loaves of bread, and eight donkey-loads of natron, used for soap-making and for drying the fish. These provisions are expected to be shared amongst the whole village, and everyone co-operates to prepare the food for the public festivities.

The oxen are slaughtered and roasted on a spit in the center of the village, as a household kitchen is not big enough to cook an entire ox. The fish are gutted and dried in salt on the house roofs, preserving them for a short while. Do not be surprised at the overwhelming smells of cooking during festival time. Anything that is not consumed at such a feast is sold at market.

SEX AND PROSTITUTION

AS IS THE CASE IN THE REST OF THE KNOWN WORLD, PROSTITUTES AND BROTHELS EXIST IN THEBES; HOWEVER, IN EGYPT THE SEX INDUSTRY IS VERY LOW KEY, AND IT IS THEREFORE DIFFICULT TO PINPOINT WHERE TO GO FOR THIS TYPE OF ENTERTAINMENT. IN A METROPOLITAN CITY, SUCH AS THEBES OR MEMPHIS, WOMEN WILL BE AVAILABLE FOR HIRE, IT IS JUST A CASE OF KNOWING WHERE TO LOOK.

Some professional dancers and singers may perform sexual favors for payment, but it will not pay to proposition such a lady unless you are certain of what she is offering—that her routines and the costumes are erotic by nature is not always an indication that more is on offer.

Rumors abound in Thebes of "sacred prostitutes"—priestesses who perform sexual acts on the statues of the gods, almost as if they were performing them on

behalf of the gods themselves. One such priestess's title is the "Hand of Atum"—the story of the creation tells how the god Atum masturbated in order to create the next generation of gods. What the "Hand of Atum" is truly required to do in the name of her job is unknown, but rumors are rife. The "God's Wife of Amun" is another religious title to which sexual connotations have been attached, although again the truth of the matter is impossible

THE OTHERS

Hearsay would suggest that within the workers' village, known locally as the "Place of Truth," and also possibly at the site of Abdju, are a group of women known as "the others" who are probably prostitutes. "The others" are single women who live together without husbands, some having children. However, unlike in some other societies, these women are accepted as legitimate members of the community, and due to the relaxed nature of sexuality in Egypt, although marriage is considered preferable, it is not a prerequisite of sexual activity.

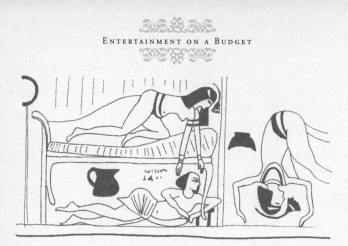

A popular comic-erotic papyrus shows an elderly client of prostitutes hiding beneath the bed.

to know, as the functions of her role are kept secret. However, one question that does arise in relation to these religious titles is whether the payment that these priestesses receive is for their religious role in general or for their sexual acts in particular; and if the former is the case then can they really be classed as prostitutes?

READING MATTER

An erotic cartoon papyrus is currently doing the rounds in Thebes—it concerns a brothel and illustrates some of the activities carried out there. The clients are a series of lower-class elderly men identified by their differing balding heads and their loincloths, which are opened at the front and hanging down at the back in a most undignified manner. They all have outsized members and are entertaining the young, nubile

ladies in various positions, some of them most unlikely-looking. One particularly amusing scene shows one of the elderly clients hiding, for want of a better word, beneath the bed due to exhaustion. The prostitute is peering over the edge of the bed desperately trying to coax him to return. Should you get the chance to read a copy, then it is certain to provide you with a few laughs; although, it must be said, it is not for the eyes of the young or the prudish!

One aspect of the sexual transaction not disclosed on the erotic papyrus is the payment at the end (or at the beginning, depending on the woman). This is something that obviously needs to be negotiated between the client and the woman, but bear in mind she is unlikely to want paying in copper, but rather in goods such as linen, jewelry, food, or livestock.

5

PRACTICAL
CONSIDERATIONS

Although the Egyptians are very accommodating, it is always useful to know the basics of how to get about the town and the wider country, where to stay, where to go for the best souvenirs, and what food is available. This chapter provides all the information required to make your visit run smoothly.

HOW TO GET THERE

THE EASIEST WAY TO TRAVEL LONG DISTANCES IS BY RIVER, AND THERE ARE NUMEROUS BOATS FOR HIRE ALONG THE NILE. DEPENDING ON WHERE YOU WANT TO TRAVEL, DIFFERENT BOATS ARE AVAILABLE; LARGE SEAFARING VESSELS, SMALLER NILE BOATS, AND PAPYRUS BOATS FOR USE IN THE MARSHES.

SEAFARING BOATS

For traveling long distances, a large wooden merchant ship will be the easiest means of reaching Egypt. The largest ships are made of cedar wood imported from Byblos, and are over 37 cubits in length. These boats are constructed using long planks of wood lashed together with rope. As the wood and the rope get wet, the wood expands, and the rope shrinks creating a watertight surface. The gunwales are high on the seafaring vessels, which are large enough to support a number of rowers as well as a large contingent of sailors. There will be more than enough room to accommodate travelers and their baggage. These boats dock at Pr-Ramses or Mennefer, where passengers will need to continue their journeys on a smaller vessel or by donkey.

Seafaring vessels dock at Pr-Ramses and Mennefer.

Journey down the Nile on a sailboat.

NILE SAILBOATS

Smaller wooden vessels are used for traveling on the Nile, whether you are going from Mennefer to Thebes, or Thebes to Abdju. Built with river travel in mind, they are small, with oars and a sail for comfortable sailing both northward and southward along the river. Many of these smaller vessels will be papyriform in shape, resembling the papyrus skiffs, but they are safer and more durable than their papyrus counterparts.

The majority of these vessels will have a small enclosed cabin in the center of the deck enabling the travelers to keep out of the sun, and a covered canopy providing a perfect place to sit and watch the beautiful scenery and the Nile wildlife. The enclosed cabin has two or three rooms within, and the doors are placed so it is impossible to see into the cabin from the deck, giving the passengers a certain degree of privacy.

Many of the vessels hired for inter-town journeys will be accompanied by the Medjay, and to advertise their presence on board they will place their shields against the enclosed cabin, so everyone along the riverbank will know not to attack the boat. Although Egypt is generally safe, like most places it can be troubled by robbers, especially if the wealthy venture out unescorted on quiet stretches of the Nile.

GETTING AROUND TOWN

WHILE YOU ARE IN THE THEBAN REGION, MANY OF THE SIGHTS CAN BE REACHED ON FOOT, AND THIS IS IN FACT THE FAVORED MODE OF TRANSPORT FOR THE LOCALS. YOU WILL NOTICE THAT MANY PEOPLE DO NOT WEAR SHOES AND ARE USED TO WALKING BAREFOOT. IF SOMEONE IS WEARING SHOES IT IS OFTEN A SIGN OF STATUS, AS IT SHOWS THEY DO NOT WALK FAR, AND THEREFORE THEIR SOFT FEET NEED PROTECTION. HOWEVER, IT IS ADVISABLE, ESPECIALLY WHEN WALKING IN THE DESERT ON THE WEST BANK, TO PROTECT YOUR FEET AGAINST ITS SCORPIONS AND SNAKES.

Rather than walk, it is possible to hire a carrying chair, which requires two men (or four if you are of a larger build), but this can be costly. These chairs comprise a low box with a raised back and sides, within which the traveler can recline on cushions, sit cross-legged, or even sit on a small stool. It takes some practice to travel comfortably, but it is widely thought to be a great display of status and wealth.

For longer journeys it is advisable to hire a donkey. In general the locals use donkeys as a beast of burden and will not often be seen riding them, but most owners will be happy to hire them out for an agreed price. Some donkeys are available with a litter attached to their backs, allowing the traveler to sit in some degree of dignity. That said, the donkey is not the most comfortable way to travel.

THE CHARIOT

The chariot is by far the most common form of transport around the major cities. The chariots used in Thebes are lightweight, with four-spoked wheels. The frames are made of wood, covered with reeds or leather.

These chariots carry two people. In a military context it would be the driver and archer, whereas to travel around the city they carry a driver and one passenger. The

A carrying chair is a sign of luxury.

THE INTRODUCTION OF THE HORSE

Although donkeys are common in Egypt, the horse is also used for transportation. Whereas the donkey is a beast of burden the horse is a rather elite animal. It was only introduced just prior to the reign of Ahmose, who used horses in his campaign to expel the Heqa Haswt from Egypt. Gradually, over the last century, the Egyptian nobility has acquired the habit of training in horsemanship skills from a young age.

Although horses are most often used to pull chariots, it is certainly not unusual to see a member of the nobility riding on horseback. The horse is equipped with a blanket thrown over its back to make it more comfortable for the rider, as well as a bridle and reins for greater control.

vehicle is pulled by two horses, and it should be considered that balance and strength are needed to ride long distances.

PAPYRUS SKIFFS

Papyrus boats are good for short journeys, perhaps across the Nile or into the papyrus marshes. You need to ensure the papyrus is still green on the boat you choose, as this will indicate it is new. They have a lifespan of only two months, and start to leak as they get older.

The papyrus boats are more like rafts, with no enclosing gunwales, and they taper in at each end. These boats come in different sizes, with the largest boasting as many as a dozen oars on each side.

The skiffs used in the marshes have a wooden-reinforced deck and only hold two or three people but are a little more stable, allowing freedom of movement. These are by far the safest means of travel on the Nile, and are known locally to be ignored by crocodiles.

A basic papyrus skiff.

ACCOMMODATION

THEBES IS A BUSY CITY SO IT MAY BE TRICKY TO FIND
ACCOMMODATION, ESPECIALLY AS THERE ARE NO OFFICIAL
HOTELS OR INNS. IT IS THEREFORE ESSENTIAL TO FIND A
FAMILY WILLING TO RENT YOU A ROOM OR SUITE, SO HEAD TO
THE OPEN VILLAGE SQUARES AND MAKE ENQUIRIES THERE.
FAMILIES IN EGYPT ARE LARGE AND THE HOUSES SMALL,
SO SPACE IS OFTEN CRAMPED. DON'T BE DISHEARTENED,
THOUGH, AS ACCOMMODATION IS OF GOOD QUALITY AND YOU
WILL BE TREATED AS A MEMBER OF THE FAMILY.

Homes in Egypt are very basic in style, the average house consisting of four or five rooms, a kitchen, and a flat roof. The houses are all built of mud brick, with wooden poles covered in reeds and mud forming the roof. Some homes have an upper floor reached by a stone staircase, often outside the building to save room within the structure. There are three types of accommodation available; barracks, large mansions, or small village houses.

BARRACKS

For the military and some of the temporary workmen there are galleried barracks. For part of the year, however, these barracks are empty and perfectly suited for short-term accommodation.

Each gallery sleeps up to 40 men on raised platforms. These galleries are entered by an off-axis doorway which leads to a columned, open area at the front and then large, private quarters at the back (which house the overseer) with a cooking area to the rear.

There is a large dining area adjacent to the sleeping quarters consisting of a pillared hall full of built-in mud-brick benches. Barracks, although basic, are ideal for groups intending to hunt or fish, as there are large kitchens to prepare the day's catch. It is also possible to hire a local family to organize the sleeping areas and to prepare and cook food.

RENTING A PROPERTY

Travelers who want a little luxury should hire a room within the town center. The average town house is small and basic, while larger houses may have a series of small rooms, magazines, and larger columned rooms facing interior courtyards.

Most houses open onto the street and are of one story with a

The local meeting area is the best place to find accommodation.

staircase leading to a flat roof. They also have cellars for storage, and in some instances for the burial of infants. The houses are whitewashed and the doors painted red.

Smaller village houses follow a general pattern consisting of four rooms with the first room opening onto the street, and a flat roof used as storage or extra sleeping space.

This first room is also used as the place of worship, while the second will have a large platform in the center, covered in cushions and used for seating during the day and as a bed at night. High windows let in light, and often there is access to a cellar for storage. The third room serves as a work area, storeroom and sleeping area for the women, and this is likely to be the room rented out to travelers.

The kitchen is at the back of the house in a walled but open area, with a clay oven and a silo for storing excess grain.

Some tourists may desire more luxurious accommodation. If this is the case, then why not rent a suite

in an elite mansion? Mansions can be of any size, but are made up of a number of smaller suites that each follow the layout of the small village houses. The main living areas of a large elite house will be arranged around an open courtyard with a pool of water in the center and a colonnade at the edge.

The bathing areas in each suite consist of either a shower room or a bath. There are also beautiful painted murals in many rooms and colored tiles and mosaics on the floors that give a sense of great luxury.

CAMPING OUT

For the truly adventurous, why not camp in the desert surrounding the Nile Valley? Tents are widely available and made from leather, wool, or thick linen draped over wooden poles. It is not advisable to camp alone, but rather hire some local Bedouin guides who will provide suitable tents, prevent you from getting lost, and advise on natural wells.

MANNERS AND CUSTOMS

THE EGYPTIANS ARE STICKLERS FOR MANNERS, APPROPRIATE BEHAVIOR, AND KNOWING YOUR PLACE. THERE ARE A NUMBER OF TEXTS DOING THE ROUNDS KNOWN AS "INSTRUCTIONS," WHICH ARE GENERALLY WRITTEN BY FATHERS ADVISING THEIR SONS ON APPROPRIATE BEHAVIOR.

These "instructions" are clear on matters such as eating in company, where it is considered particularly bad-mannered to overeat. A guest should eat sparingly, and should not be a glutton who pounces on the food as soon as it is served. It is, however, considered rude to refuse anything offered by the host.

DRINKING

Although it is acceptable to drink beer and wine, and in fact the former is a staple of the Egyptian diet, it is not acceptable to drink to excess, as it is believed that alcohol will make a fool of the most sensible man and causes people to speak ill of others. Drunkards are abhorred in society, and no one will hold out a hand to help someone who has fallen under the influence— therefore drinking alcohol should be kept to a minimum.

COMPORTMENT

It is considered desirable for a good law-abiding citizen to be quiet and timid, and it is thought that this type of person attracts benefits. It is also considered polite to speak only when addressed, especially if you are in the company of superiors, and then try to be as inoffensive as possible.

It is considered uncouth to be boastful or antagonistic, and this will result in aggression. Should you come across a fight, then you should not intervene, as self-restraint is admired above all else; even in an argument amongst friends and equals it is considered best not to participate, as "silence will serve you well."

DISCRETION

Discretion is also a favored trait, while gossip is in turn discouraged. Anything that is seen or heard in the houses of friends or acquaintances should be kept confidential. Once invited into someone's house, the guest should be respectful, should not snoop, and should not discuss the contents of the home outside. It is essential therefore to earn trust and try to maintain this through any means possible.

The intelligent in society should certainly not act superior to those who have not had the benefit of their education, and should consult both the educated and uneducated alike for advice, as it is thought that good advice and wisdom can be found in the most surprising places. Therefore everyone should be treated with respect.

TIPS FOR THE TRAVELER

As a visitor it is best to be polite and friendly to all; greet people you meet, and introduce yourself and answer their questions without hesitation. Remember that one of the main laws of Egypt is that of Maat—cosmic balance or truth—and therefore it is best to be truthful or be silent.

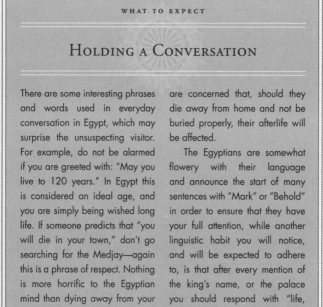

WHAT TO EXPECT

HOLDING A CONVERSATION

There are some interesting phrases and words used in everyday conversation in Egypt, which may surprise the unsuspecting visitor. For example, do not be alarmed if you are greeted with: "May you live to 120 years." In Egypt this is considered an ideal age, and you are simply being wished long life. If someone predicts that "you will die in your town," don't go searching for the Medjay—again this is a phrase of respect. Nothing is more horrific to the Egyptian mind than dying away from your town, your family and friends. As the Egyptians have such distinctive burial practices, they are concerned that, should they die away from home and not be buried properly, their afterlife will be affected.

The Egyptians are somewhat flowery with their language and announce the start of many sentences with "Mark" or "Behold" in order to ensure that they have your full attention, while another linguistic habit you will notice, and will be expected to adhere to, is that after every mention of the king's name, or the palace you should respond with "life, prosperity, and health" as a sign of respect and goodwill to the divine ruler.

CLOTHING AND DRESS

THE EGYPTIAN CLIMATE BEING WHAT IT IS, EGYPTIAN FASHIONS ARE CENTERED ON BEING COOL, AND THEREFORE THE ONLY FABRIC THEY WEAR IS LINEN. NORMALLY THE LINEN REMAINS ITS NATURAL COLOR, WHICH VARIES FROM WHITE TO A GOLDEN-BROWN COLOR DEPENDING ON THE MATURITY OF THE FLAX USED TO PRODUCE IT. LINEN IS EXPENSIVE TO DYE AND IT IS IMPOSSIBLE TO MAKE THE COLOR FAST, MEANING IT WILL GRADUALLY FADE.

Although there are various accessories to be added to that must-have outfit in the form of colored or tapestry sashes, pleated shawls or jewelry, the basic item of clothing worn by both men and women is the tunic: a T-shaped garment, either waist-length or floor-length depending on personal choice. Many of these tunics have removable sleeves for the summer, and thicker linen is used for winter tunics against the cold evenings.

Waist-length tunics are worn with calf-length kilts, which consist of a simple rectangular piece of fabric wrapped around the body and gathered at the front to create a full, cascading effect, although the front is often shorter than the back. The fashion at present is for volume – so the more fabric you can incorporate into your kilts or shawls the richer and more fashionable you will seem. Kilts are held in place with a sash, often

Traditional Egyptian dress: a basic tunic for men, and a longer tunic with a pleated shawl for women.

brightly colored with a fringe or a trim—standing out against the stark white of the kilt or tunic. Women will wear sashes, which fall down to the floor, holding in place their shawls or the elaborate folds of their tunics.

Although the tunics are plain in design, there are ways of making them more elaborate with the aid of pleats and folds, either across the bodice and sleeves or in the skirt. However, the easiest way of making the tunic unique is with accessories. Women will often tie a pleated shawl around the shoulders of their tunic in a complicated fashion, creating interesting neckline folds or even full sleeves—all with a rectangle of material. These shawls are often decorated with a trim or fringe, or sometimes embroidered with colored designs; the most expensive shawls are appliquéd with beads and rosettes.

Many of the highest-quality tunics are also decorated with tapestry designs, actually forming part of the fabric, which are used as trims around the open neck, the hem, or the sleeves. Collars are also often added to a plain tunic—generally they are also of linen, but are decorated with tapestry, embroidery, or beads. These are stitched to the tunic and then removed when it is taken to be cleaned.

HEADGEAR

To protect the head from the harsh heat the Egyptians often wear headcloths, and this is recommended for all visitors. Do not be surprised, however, that the majority of the Egyptians you meet have shaved heads as a precaution against lice, and therefore need to protect the sensitive scalp from the sun. Most people wear a simple headcloth made of a rectangle or semi-circle of linen (known as a *khat* headdress), draped over the head and neck, and tied in place with a linen band. These headcloths are always white, as it reflects the heat, although the wealthy sometimes have colored or embroidered trims.

FOOTWEAR

Basic sandals are also in vogue in Thebes at the moment, with very little difference between those of men and women. The most expensive are made of papyrus or leather, and the most common are made of simple Nile reeds. They are simple in design, with a thong that goes between the toes and a strap over the foot, enabling the feet to breathe. For something a little bit different, why not dye the reeds to create colored shoes? Although the color will not last long, it will create a lovely finish to your Egyptian outfit.

FOOD AND DRINK

IT IS NOT DIFFICULT TO EAT IN THEBES, BUT THERE ARE NO SUCH THINGS AS INNS OR RESTAURANTS. HOWEVER, SOME HOMES OPEN THEIR DOORS TO TRAVELERS PROVIDING A HOME-COOKED MEAL AND FRESH BEVERAGES. ALTHOUGH NO OFFICIAL SIGNAGE IS USED, IT IS ALWAYS MADE CLEAR WHICH HOUSES IN THE TOWN ARE WELCOMING GUESTS. IT IS ALSO EASY TO BUY FOOD SUCH AS DRIED FISH, FRUIT, BREAD, AND BEER IN THE PUBLIC SQUARE FOR A SMALL FEE—HOME-PREPARED BY THE WOMEN OF THE VILLAGES.

Food in Egypt is generally simple. It often consists of fish and vegetables, and these are served with a variety of sauces that add extra flavor and texture.

The staple food, however, is bread made from emmer wheat.

Because the flour is ground with a stone against a stone slab, the bread can sometimes seem a little coarse to the foreign palate. The loaves that are made are sold moulded into different shapes to indicate their ingredients, as there

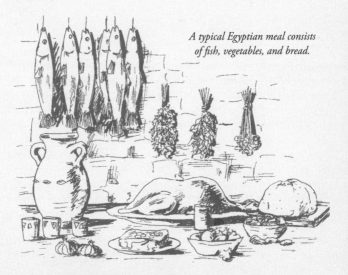

A typical Egyptian meal consists of fish, vegetables, and bread.

are a number of different-flavored breads on the market, including honey and date breads.

Most Egyptians will not eat a great deal of meat in their diet but the wealthy tourist will be able to obtain beef and duck in addition to the lower-quality meat including pork and fowl. Meat is mostly roasted over an open fire, and the fat is used in the sauces. Sauces for the meat also include chick peas, honey, dates, and pomegranates flavored with spices and garlic. More commonly you will be offered salted or dried fish to eat. The fish is caught daily in the Nile and is covered in salt and left to dry in the sun. Both fish and meat will be served with a mixture of vegetables include cucumber, lettuce, and onions.

DRINK

Another of the staples of the Egyptian diet is beer, made from partially cooked or stale barley bread or emmer wheat. This beer is more soup-like than liquid, and some can be eaten with a spoon. Known locally as *henket* this beverage is made in the households to be sold at the market or consumed by the family, or in breweries attached to the temples for official distribution as wages. For the more adventurous tourist, why not try the flavored beer? During fermentation dates, honey, and spices are added, which speeds fermentation and gives

it a distinctive flavor. This beer is alcoholic, but will not induce drunkenness unless taken in excess; it is even served to children as part of their daily diet.

An alternative to beer is red or white wine, a far superior beverage. There are numerous vineyards in Thebes, and it may be possible to go on a tour of one of these and try their different blends of grapes. Some of the best-known vineyards, however, are in the Kharga and Dakla oases, although imported wines from Syria are particularly favored amongst the Theban and Pr-Ramses elite; these are made from dates and pomegranates rather than grapes. The best wines are those that have fermented for several years, and some vineyards will also add honey and spices to the wine to add flavor. Egyptian wine is favored by many foreigners, although it may have a slightly oily aftertaste to those not used to it. If wine is a little oily, add some water to eliminate this—although the Egyptians do not do this.

Very popular in the royal household is *shedeh*, a drink very similar to wine, made with red grapes and served warm; it is a particularly refreshing spiced drink for the winter nights. Shedeh is very expensive and rare, so if you have the opportunity to sample it it is advisable to accept. However, like all alcoholic beverages it should be enjoyed responsibly.

MONEY

SHOPPING IN EGYPT CAN BE A FUN EXPERIENCE, AND IT IS SOMETHING THAT EVERY TRAVELER SHOULD TAKE THE CHANCE TO PARTICIPATE IN. THE EGYPTIAN ECONOMY IS BASED ON BARTERING, AND THEREFORE YOU WILL NEED TO TAKE A GOOD SUPPLY OF GOODS WITH YOU IN ORDER TO EXCHANGE THEM FOR ALL THE ITEMS THAT YOU WANT. THIS MAKES FOR A COMPLEX EXCHANGE SYSTEM, SO SHOPPING CAN TAKE A WHILE. DON'T EXPECT TO POP OUT FOR A SHORT TRIP—IT CAN TAKE ALL AFTERNOON JUST TO PURCHASE TWO OR THREE ITEMS.

There is no such place as a market, although if you make your way toward the shore of the Nile, the harbors, or the village squares, you will find stalls where merchants and local villagers have set up to sell their goods. For certain goods it may be necessary for you to visit the craftsmen themselves, either at their workshops or their homes, and in fact many things can be made to order if you have the time to wait.

Negotiating over price is where things get complicated, as goods are swapped for other goods. However, there is a relative price measured in weights of copper or silver, known as *deben*. Most locals will be aware of the relative exchange rate, whereas a tourist may have some difficulty, so try to find out what the local rates for certain goods are.

Remember, objects are only valuable if someone wants them— so why not bring unusual items from your home country or town, perhaps even something that is unavailable in Egypt itself?

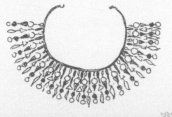

Everything is available to buy in Egypt from livestock to the finest jewelry.

THE GOING RATE

In order to prevent the unwary traveler being ripped off by wily merchants, here are some trading tips. It needs to be noted, however, that as Thebes is not on a direct trade route, it is likely to be a little more expensive than Mennefer, where the port is situated. In Mennefer the traders from far and wide can be seen selling their wares; this is not the case in Thebes, although most of the same goods are available.

CLOTHES

A linen tunic of middling quality is worth roughly 5 deben of copper or 3 hin (jars) of oil whereas a triangular loincloth will cost anything between 4 and 16 deben of copper. If you need to purchase a new pair of sandals this will cost anything up to 3 deben of copper or a low-quality loincloth.

JEWELRY

Egypt is well known for its jewelry production and it is possible to buy some relatively cheaply. However, if you want quality you need to spend more. A faience necklace is the cheapest form at 5 deben, whereas a lapis necklace will cost at least 8 deben and a gold counterpoise for a necklace will be 36 deben of copper, or even as much as a young donkey!

CONSUMABLES

Many of the goods on sale will be consumables: food, beverages, and oil. Loaves of bread are sold in bulk, with ten loaves costing 2 deben of copper or two hin of oil. A large amphora of beer will cost 2 deben, and 4 deben will buy the same amount of wine.

As it is not practical to carry around bags of copper, it is handy to know that a goat can be exchanged for the equivalent of 1–3 deben and papyrus (readily available in the north) can be exchanged for 4 deben of copper—so it is recommended that you ensure you have plenty of papyrus to bargain with, as it is much lighter to carry around with you—and perhaps have a couple of goats to hand as well.

SHOPPING

THERE ARE MANY THINGS TO BUY IN AND AROUND THEBES, FROM FOOD AND CONSUMABLES TO CLOTHES AND BURIAL GOODS. ANYTHING YOU WANT IS AVAILABLE, AND MANY THINGS CAN BE MADE TO ORDER ACCORDING TO PERSONAL SPECIFICATIONS, SO IT IS POSSIBLE TO PURCHASE SOMETHING COMPLETELY UNIQUE.

LINEN

The most common material available will be linen, as this is what most clothes are made from. However, the quality and thickness varies greatly. The finer the linen, the more expensive it is, and the finest quality will be almost transparent. For winter garments very thick linen is used, or wool can be woven into cloaks and long-sleeved tunics. The linen will primarily be undyed, but varies from white to golden-brown depending on the maturity of the flax. Although color is not often used in the main garments colored sashes or tapestry bands are made to decorate them. If colored garments are required it is possible to order them, but the dyes are not color-fast and will fade when washed.

JEWELRY

Though the clothes worn by the Egyptians are very plain, with little color or decoration, their jewelry is very elaborate, and this is something that the visitor should perhaps invest in. Jewelry comes in many forms, made of any material you can think of. If your budget does not stretch to semiprecious stones, then they can be copied in faience.

The most common piece of jewelry is the wide collar, made of a row of beads or amulets; this can be in any form (ankhs, animals,

Women examine the quality of the wares at a linen workshop.

SHOPPING FOR JEWELRY

While shopping for jewelry you need to be very clear what you want and the amount you are willing to pay for it.

The vast majority of the jewelry available will be made of faience, a colorful substance rather like clay but made from heated sand. This can be found in a variety of colors and shapes, as when warm it is malleable. However, you need to be aware that faience can be produced to resemble any semiprecious stone, almost so as to be unrecognizable—don't be caught out by fakes. If, on the other hand, you want stone jewelry, this is also available, but as many of the stones are imported it can be expensive. The cheapest stones are cornelian, amethyst, red jasper, and rock crystal, as they are available from Egypt; but the very fashionable lapis lazuli and onyx have to be imported, and this is reflected in the price.

If you desire these rocks to be mounted, or to have metal clasps or terminals, bear in mind that silver is imported and therefore more expensive than gold; an unusual alternative to both is electrum, which is a combination of the two.

fruit, or flowers) and also in any color. To counteract the weight, a counterpoise of bronze or gold is needed to hang down the back. Bracelets, armlets, and anklets can be made to match such a necklace.

Earrings come in two types, the cheaper being buttons or plugs which simply show a round shape on the earlobe. While the other, more expensive type is the dangling form, which you could perhaps have made to match the rest of your jewelry purchases.

INCENSE

One very important product of Egypt is incense. It is made locally from a combination of local produce and imported plants and tree gum. The most expensive is called *kyphi*, which is made up of 16 different ingredients including dried myrrh, juniper berries, twigs of mastic, and fenugreek. It is sold as incense pellets for scenting the home and clothes, or mixed with honey and moulded into pills and used as a breath freshener.

MEDICAL TREATMENT

UNFORTUNATELY EVERYONE FALLS ILL, AND IF THIS SHOULD HAPPEN ON YOUR TRIP THERE ARE A NUMBER OF PEOPLE YOU COULD VISIT FOR A CONSULTATION. THE EGYPTIAN PHYSICIANS ARE THE BEST IN THE WORLD, PROVIDING THE MOST EFFECTIVE TREATMENT. THE BEST, AND THEREFORE THE MOST EXPENSIVE, PHYSICIANS ARE THE PRIESTS, WHO LEARN THEIR TRADE IN THE HOUSE OF LIFE ATTACHED TO THE TEMPLES; THE BEST AND MOST FAMOUS HAVING BEEN SET UP BY THE GREAT SAGE IMHOTEP HIMSELF AT MENNEFER, ALTHOUGH THEBES ALSO BOASTS SOME TRAINING CENTERS (MAINLY AT KARNAK).

The nature of your ailment dictates who you will visit. If you have been bitten by a scorpion or snake you need to approach the priests of Selqet, who will appeal to the goddess for a cure. If, however, you have caught a plague, then the priests of Sekhmet should be approached. The priests appeal to the deities to relieve the ailment, which they themselves have caused. The cost of treatment will obviously depend on the severity of the condition. The ease of approaching the priests will also be dependent on the time of year and how busy the temple is; but if you state your case to the doorkeeper then he can approach the priests on your behalf.

If the priestly physicians are a little out of your budget, then lay physicians can be approached. These are often scribes, and you will need to enquire in the local area for the physician most suited to your particular ailment, as they all have particular specialities, including eyes, childbirth, and stings and bites. The price for treatment will be negotiable.

An Egyptian man is treated for his ailments by a "wise-woman."

MINOR AILMENTS

If your ailment is minor—cuts, abrasions, diarrhea, or headaches—then why not visit the village wise-woman? There will be a woman trained in the required skills in most villages, and it would be best to ask locally who is the most appropriate. These wise-women are often the best people to visit for issues of pregnancy and childbirth as they have lots of practice in this field.

As the skills of the physicians and wise-women are passed down through the generations, it is essential to chose someone from a long line of physicians to guarantee the best treatment.

To ensure you remain healthy, wear lots of kohl around your eyes as protection from the sun, dust, and flies, and keep your skin well anointed with oils and perfumes to prevent it drying out. Drink plenty of fluids.

EASY-TO-PRODUCE REMEDIES

While traveling in the Theban region you may become unwell, but don't necessarily want to engage the services of a physician. Many remedies for burns, indigestion, or diarrhea can be purchased in the streets.

If suffering with diarrhoea, a good local cure consists of ⅛ of a container of figs and grapes, bread dough, pit corn, fresh earth, onion, and elderberry, mixed together and taken internally until the condition clears up.

If you have indigestion, crush a hog's tooth and have it mixed into the dough of four sugar cakes. Eat for four days and the indigestion should pass—and if it doesn't, at least the cakes taste nice.

If you have burnt yourself, a compress should be made using barley bread, animal fat, and salt, mixed together and bandaged over the burn to ease the pain and lessen the inflammation.

A popular remedy in the Theban region for general aches and pains is to make use of the great sun-god Ra. The painful area is anointed with oils and then exposed to the healing rays of the sun, which will relieve the pain. Give this a go before hiring a doctor, and save yourself a hefty bill.

CRIME AND THE LAW

ALTHOUGH YOU WILL NEVER FIND THE LAWS OF EGYPT WRITTEN DOWN, THE EGYPTIANS ARE GENERALLY LAW-ABIDING CITIZENS AND THERE ARE HARSH PUNISHMENTS FOR THOSE WHO ARE NOT. THE MEDJAY ARE THE LOCAL THEBAN POLICE FORCE, AND AS SUCH ARE RESPONSIBLE PRIMARILY FOR PATROLLING THE WESTERN CEMETERIES TO PREVENT TOMB ROBBERIES. BECAUSE OF THIS THEY HAVE LITTLE TO DO WITH DAY-TO-DAY CRIME ALTHOUGH THEY ARE DEFINITELY AN EFFECTIVE ARMED PRESENCE IN THE TOWN.

Crimes are dealt with on an individual basis and are not classified crimes as such unless the victim chooses to pursue the issue. So, for example, if a theft occurs, it is dealt with officially only if the injured party reports it. Generally the thief is required to return the stolen goods, sometimes with a compensation payment—for example, if three goats are stolen the thief will need to return four.

Be warned, however, that this relatively lenient attitude does not extend to the property of the state. Should you be tempted to steal anything from the state or from a temple, you can be assured that such a crime will be investigated by the highest authority, with very severe punishments for anyone found guilty.

TRIAL BY JURY

The cases that are serious enough to be pursued officially are addressed by the *kenbet* or court, consisting of 16 local individuals and the vizier. Although they aim to discover the truth, the kenbet primarily maintains public order, and often punishments are given

A physical beating is a common form of punishment administered by the courts.

according to the general public opinion. If, however, someone lies in the kenbet, they are put on trial themselves for perjury, which can result in the death penalty.

Should you find yourself in the kenbet as the accused, it is possible to bribe the vizier so the case swings in your favor; or simply to swear that you will not offend again, which is the most common way to end a case. However, this is not a promise to be given lightly, as if this oath should be broken the penalties are very high indeed.

SENTENCING

Being tried at the kenbet is a very serious thing, as the vizier has the power to destroy not only the defendant but his entire family. It is not uncommon for certain crimes to be punished by loss of occupation for the defendant and his descendants. In some instances a criminal and his family can be sentenced to lifelong labor as one of the state-owned laborers—a terrible punishment, as the whole family is often sent to the mines or the quarries. Even the journey there is dangerous, and many families die before they reach their destination. However, this punishment only works one way, as a husband cannot be punished for the crimes of his wife.

Other penalties for a range of minor through to major crimes are not always as harsh, although they are still unpleasant. There is little consistency between the crime and the punishment, but favored forms are lashes with a whip (normally in multiples of ten) for certain minor misdemeanors, increasing to up to five open wounds inflicted with a knife, or mutilation by having the nose and ears cut off. This latter punishment is often administered to women who commit adultery at the behest of their cuckolded husbands.

Major crimes such as murder, tomb robbery, or any crime against the king or the state are punished with the death penalty, either by impaling on a sharp stick through the stomach—a slow, agonizing death—or being burnt alive, often publicly so as to act as a deterrent.

If a criminal is executed he is denied burial, which denies him an afterlife; in some instances this is taken further, with the erasure or the changing of his name so it will never be repeated after death, ensuring there will be no rebirth.

As each crime is addressed individually, so the punishment often fits the crime. However, the injured party may wish to pursue the matter further, pushing for the harshest punishment possible, even if it is out of proportion to the crime. So if at all possible it is best not to end up in the law court at all.

WORKING AND STUDYING

THE EGYPTIANS ARE A VERY HARD-WORKING NATION, WITH THE MEN WORKING DAYLIGHT HOURS FOR TEN DAYS AT A TIME BEFORE HAVING TWO DAYS OFF. THIS WORKING PATTERN IS FOLLOWED REGARDLESS OF STATUS, ALTHOUGH THE MILITARY ON EXPEDITIONS (EITHER TRADING OR CAMPAIGNING) WILL WORK FOR LONGER PERIODS WITHOUT A REST DAY.

During the working week most of the villages will be devoid of men, who have gone to work, leaving just the women, children, and the elderly carrying out all the household tasks. Some of the women however also work, either in the home producing clothes, sandals, bread, and beer to take to market, or as a housekeeper or servant in an elite household.

There are numerous occupations that a man can go into, and a text known locally as the *Satire of the Trades* describes in a no-holds-barred manner the different opportunities available.

"The barber barbers till nightfall,
He betakes himself to town,
He sets himself up in his corner,
He moves from street to street
Looking for someone to barber.

The gardener carries a yoke,
His shoulders are bent as
    with age;
There's a swelling on his neck,
And it festers.

The courier goes into the desert,
Leaving his goods to his
    children;
Fearful of lions and Asiatics,
He knows himself only when he
    is in Egypt."

The text is designed to show that scribedom is the best profession to enter: "It's the greatest of all callings, there's none like it in the land." However, not many people can become scribes, as less than one percent of the population is literate. Schooling for those who choose this career is intense, starting at five years old. The children acquire the skill through learning ancient texts by rote and copying "model letters" that are perfect in grammar, structure, and content.

Although scribes work hard, many of them spend their spare time writing literary texts such as *The Shipwrecked Sailor* (a tale of high seas and adventure), the *Five Tales of Wonder* (tales of magic and wonderment) as well as erotic love poetry, and "Instructions" giving advice on good living, etiquette, and manners. It is rumored that there is a scribe at the Place of Truth in Thebes who is in the process of writing a dream interpretation book—the first outside a temple environment. Perhaps a lucky traveler will get the opportunity to meet him and to consult him on their dreams.

A scribe writes cursive script upon his papyrus.

WAGES

While traveling, it is always good to be aware that pay day is on the 28th day of every month, so this is the time of frivolity and increased activity in the markets. Wages are paid not in copper but in quantities of grain—a specified amount for different positions.

Someone on a high salary earns approximately 5.5 *khar* of grain per month, enough to feed a family of 10 to 15. For those with small families this means there is an excess, which can be traded for other goods at the market, increasing wealth, or improving diet and lifestyle. Normally people with larger families have these wages supplemented by other members of the family who are also working. It is unusual for a large extended family to have only one person bringing home an income.

For those working for the state the government supplies other basic goods such as housing, firewood, fish, vegetables, water, and oil in addition to these wages. Extra rations are also given to state employees during religious festivals, or as a bonus if they please the king.

REFERENCES AND RESOURCES

If you require further information for your trip to Egypt, why not consult some of the Egyptian literary works which may give insight into the Egyptian mind, beliefs, and mannerisms? In this section you will also discover some hieroglyphs to help you identify the builders of certain monuments and the deities worshipped in the temples.

RULERS OF EGYPT

IN THE LAST 2,000 OR SO YEARS OF EGYPTIAN HISTORY THERE HAVE BEEN HUNDREDS OF KINGS—FAR TOO MANY TO LIST HERE. HOWEVER, HERE ARE THE NAMES OF THE DYNASTIES AND THEIR MOST IMPORTANT SOVEREIGNS.

PREDYNASTIC EGYPT

From the creation, Egypt was ruled by gods—indeed it still is, as a series of god-kings have taken the throne. The first true king of all Egypt, however, was Narmer, who united Lower and Upper Egypt a little under 2,000 years ago.

EARLY DYNASTIC PERIOD

Following the unification of Egypt under Narmer, the Early Dynastic Period takes in the rule of the First Dynasty, which held power for around 200 years. Then the Second Dynasty held sway for around another 200 years.

THE OLD KINGDOM

The ascent of the Third Dynasty some 1,500 years ago brought with it the great king Djoser, the builder of the step pyramid at Saqqara.

The Old Kingdom reached the peak of its power with the rise of the Fourth Dynasty under Snefru, the great pyramid builder, some 1,300 years ago. His successor Khufu built the Great Pyramid at Giza. The weakening of central power under the Fifth Dynasty saw the decline of the Old Kingdom, with increasing famine and civil conflict.

The last dynasty of the Old Kingdom was the Sixth Dynasty, which arose some 1,100 years ago. The 160-year reign of its kings Tety, Pepy Meryre, Merenre Nemtyemzaf, and Pepy Neferkara saw the rising power of the nobility, and the relative decline of royal power.

THE FIRST INTERMEDIATE PERIOD

Under the Sixth Dynasty, the nation of Egypt became divided once more.

The records from the era are poor, but Egypt remained divided under the Seventh and Eighth Dynasties. Then, about 900 years ago, the rise of the Ninth and Tenth Dynasties reunited Lower (northern) Egypt; while in the south the Eleventh Dynasty reunited Upper Egypt, with Thebes as its capital.

The resulting clash brought the Eleventh Dynasty to power over the whole of Egypt, and as a

result saw the rise of the era of the Middle Kingdom.

THE MIDDLE KINGDOM

The era of the Middle Kingdom arose around 800 years ago during the Eleventh Dynasty. Mentuhotep Nebhetepre was the first ruler to reunite Upper and Lower Egypt; however, he was still reliant on the assistance of local governors, and it wasn't until the reign of Senusret Khakhaure some 200 years later that the power of the king was once again absolute.

A smooth transition to the rule of the Twelfth Dynasty took place around 750 years ago with the rule of Amenemhat I. His successors bolstered Egypt's military might, with Amenemhet Nymaatra fortifying the northern borders, and the later Senusret Kheperkara and Senusret Khakhaura extending Egypt's southern lands into Nubia and building a number of fortresses.

THE SECOND INTERMEDIATE PERIOD

A period of relative weakness and division for the nation of Egypt began some five and a half centuries ago with the ascent of the Thirteenth Dynasty to the throne. The weak ruling family lost power in the south to the Nubian Fourteenth Dynasty, and eventually the Asiatic Heqa Haswt took advantage of this to invade and found the Fifteenth Dynasty around a century later.

Egypt remained divided under the kings of the Sixteenth and Seventeenth dynasties until Seqenenre Tao (the father of Amhose Nebpehtyre) and his first son Kamose began the wars that would eventually rid Egypt of its Heqa Haswt rulers and lead to its reunification.

THE NEW KINGDOM

Beginning with the reign of Ahmose Nebpehtyre around 400 years ago, Egypt was reunited and reborn in the era of the Eighteenth Dynasty. The greatest king of the era was Thutmosis Menkheperre, who ruled for over 50 years until some two and a half centuries ago. The dynasty also included a number of other great kings such as Tutankhamun Nebkheperure. It concluded with the reign of Horemheb Djeserkheperure, who bequeathed power to the first king of the current dynasty a little under a hundred years ago.

The Nineteenth Dynasty, the reigning dynasty, began with the rule of Ramses I, who was followed by Sety Menmaatra, and now the current king Ramses II.

RECOMMENDED READING

WHATEVER THE REASON FOR YOUR VISIT TO THEBES, INDULGING IN A LITTLE BACKGROUND READING IS SURE TO ENHANCE YOUR UNDERSTANDING OF BOTH THE PLACE AND ITS PEOPLE, AND THEREBY HELP YOU ENJOY YOUR TRIP MORE.

SATIRE OF THE TRADES

Written some 500 years ago, this is an amusing text that describes the woes of many occupations held in Egypt.

TALES OF WONDER

Although written around 500 years ago these five tales are set in the Pyramid Age. They take place in the royal court, where a prince is telling his father Khufu magical tales of kings past.

THE SHIPWRECKED SAILOR

A tale of adventure on high seas where the poor shipwrecked sailor is washed up on a deserted island, with nothing but a giant talking snake for company.

WISDOM TEXTS

There is a collection of these in circulation, giving advice on the correct etiquette for day-to-day living. The newest one is the instruction of Amenemope to his son on the merits of being a good scholar and leading a good life.

LOVE SONGS

These can be heard sung and recited in the streets of most large towns, but circulating in Thebes are written copies of these poems of love. Although they may seem to be about trivial matters, they are written with the greatest of scholarly talent.

An extract from the Book of the Dead.

What to Expect

Commissioning a Burial Text

If whilst in Thebes you decide to have a copy of the *Spells for Going Forth by Day* commissioned for your own burial, then there are numerous options depending on time and finance. You can have the sacred texts produced on a variety of objects: boxes, coffins, papyrus or if you are very wealthy a hypocephalus, a rare disk-shaped object that only uses spell 162, but is used for only the most special burials.

The most common commission, however, is a papyrus, either monochrome with cursive script or in hieroglyphic script with colorful vignettes. Workshops dotted throughout the Theban region can provide custom-made paypyri, allowing you to choose which chapters of the text you would like included—so do your research beforehand. Alternatively, "off the peg" versions are available for those on a budget, to which the artists will simply add your name and titles by way of personalization. Prices depend on the sophistication of the finished object.

BOOK OF THE AMDUAT AND BOOK OF GATES

These are collections of twelve texts following the twelve hours of the nocturnal journey of the sun god. Both are highly illustrated and very beautiful.

LITANY OF RE

This is another religious text connected with the solar god and the funerary cult. This text lists the 72 forms of the sun god, enabling the deceased to appeal to any aspect of this deity on his nocturnal journey.

BOOK OF THE DEAD (SPELLS FOR GOING FORTH BY DAY)

There are hundreds of copies of this in circulation (see left) and it is possible to get a personal copy commissioned. Not a book for general reading, it is rather a collection of religious spells that are designed to protect the deceased in the afterlife.

Useful Hieroglyphs

As the majority of Egyptians are not literate it is not especially important to be able to read the hieroglyphic language during your trip; however, it can prove enlightening. The hieroglyphic script is used primarily in temples and tombs, whereas everyday accounts and records are written in a shorthand version known as hieratic (or cursive).

To learn hieroglyphs is a complicated process as each sign (and there are over 700 of them) has a different phonetic value, and can also be used either alone to represent an entire word, or in combination with others to spell out a word letter by letter. However, an understanding of hieroglyphs is certain to make your trip more enjoyable so the following is a list of words that you may need in your day-to-day dealings. However, you should not expect someone in the market selling bread to be able to read the word, so it is more important that you are able to pronounce it too.

WORD	SOUND	HIEROGLYPHICS
Water	Moo	
Beer	Henqet	
Wine	Eerip	
Vegetables	Renpoot	
Bread	Tee	
Fowl	Aped-oo	
Oxen	Ka-oo	
Fig	Daboo	
Cucumber	Shespet	
Husband	He	
Wife	Humet	
Mother	Moot	
Father	It	
Egypt	Kemet	

NAMES OF THE GODS

When you are visiting tombs and temples you will often note the name of the god written above the image; so it helps to be able to recognize the spelling of the most common gods. There are hundreds of gods in the pantheon and many of their names are a combination of more than one name.

GOD	HIEROGLYPHICS	ROLE
Amun		Solar god and god of Thebes.
Mut		Consort of Amun, sometimes shown with a lioness head.
Khonsu		Lunar god and son of Amun and Mut.
Re-Horakhty		A solar deity, a combination of Ra and Horus. Shown with a hawk head.
Osiris		God of the Underworld.
Isis		Mother goddess, and sister/wife of Osiris.
Horus		God of order, the son of Osiris and Isis and the king is the living incarnation of this god.
Seth		God of chaos, shown with the head of an unknown animal.
Hathor		Mother goddess, shown as a cow or with a cow's head.
Nut		Sky goddess, often shown on the inside of coffins.

WHAT TO EXPECT

SCRIBAL SCHOOL

There is a per ankh (House of Life) or scribal training school situated at the Ramesseum (Khnemet), that trains potential priests, physicians and nobles, and perhaps royal children. The lector priest teaches the young boys basic hieratic signs, then the priest reads classical texts to them and the young boys write them down. This institution also produces copies of the *Book of the Dead* for purchase, as well as other religious texts for circulation within the religious community.

For the visitor looking to educate a son, and place him on the path of a career within the temple personnel, it may be worth negotiating a price with the lector priest of this impressive institution.

USEFUL TERMS AND PHRASES

THERE ARE A NUMBER OF COMMON WORDS AND PHRASES YOU WILL HEAR THROUGHOUT YOUR TRIP THAT YOU FEEL MAY NEED CLARIFYING. THESE ARE PRESENTED HERE IN ALPHABETICAL ORDER AND SHOULD HELP YOU WHILST SITE SEEING TO IDENTIFY ARCHITECTURAL ELEMENTS, RELIGIOUS ICONS, AND BELIEFS AS WELL AS OTHER LOCAL TERMS THAT YOU MAY COME ACROSS. ALSO IN THIS SECTION YOU WILL FIND A NUMBER OF USEFUL PHRASES IN EGYPTIAN, WHICH CAN MAKE DAY-TO-DAY TRANSACTIONS SOMEWHAT EASIER.

USEFUL WORDS

Aamw *Asiatics—the people who come from the land to the East of Egypt past the Red Sea*

Amduat *the term used by the Egyptians to refer to the afterlife, the place the deceased are reborn into for eternity.*

Benben stone *the pyramid-shaped stone at the top of pyramids and obelisks reminiscent of the shape of the mound of creation and the start of all life.*

Canopic jars *four jars that are placed into the tomb and are used to hold the desiccated internal organs of the deceased.*

Cubit *the official measurement used in Egypt which corresponds roughly with the distance between the elbow and the end of the fingertips.*

Deben *a weight of copper or silver against which a standardization of market prices are set.*

Hall of Judgment *the place where the deceased will meet the god of the Underworld, and have their hearts weighed against Maat the goddess of truth before being admitted into the Underworld.*

Hapy *the annual flooding of the Nile which is essential for the irrigation of the land and the fertility of the soil.*

Heb sed *the heb festival carried out every 30 years by the king to prove he is eligible to continue ruling. The run is the most important part where he has to run around set markers representing the length and breadth of Egypt.*

Heqa Haswt *the name of the Asiatics from the Syro-Palestinian region who gained control of Egypt for 100 years before being expelled by Ahmose Nebpehttyra.*

Hin *a measurement of liquid, which like the deben is used as a standardization for market prices.*

Hypocephalus *a circular piece of papyrus or bronze placed behind the head of the mummy. The spell from the Book of the Dead written on it will warm the head aiding with rebirth.*

Ka *the human spirit, which needs to be nourished with food and drink in the afterlife, in order for it to be reborn.*

Lower Egypt *the name given to north Egypt from Mennefer to the Great Green (Mediterranean Sea).*

Maat (Law of) *the religious law in Egypt is set by Maat, the goddess of truth and justice. If her law is upheld the equilibrium of the universe is balanced, whereas if it is not the universe will plunge into primordial chaos.*

Mastaba *a bench-shaped superstructure over the burials of the nobles in the Pyramid Age and royalty in the time of the unification.*

Medjay *the police force of Egypt. Their name comes from a Nubian tribe who initially held the post; but now any fit young man can be a Medjay.*

Natron *the natural salt from the Wadi Natron which is used in the mummification process, also used in cooking and as soap.*

Negative Confession *in the Hall of Judgment the deceased must make the negative confession before the 42 judges of the dead, explaining all the things that they have not done.*

Nine Bows *the symbolic name given to the traditional enemies of Egypt, often represented on footstools and sandals as bows lying in a row.*

Nomarch *the local ruler of a nome.*

Nome *one of 42 regions in Egypt, small areas governed by a local ruler with a capital city, local temple, and religious cult.*

Obelisk *a tall stone monument topped with a benben stone, inscribed with prayers to the sun-god.*

Osiride pillars *are pillars carved to look like the mummified god of the Underworld, Osiris.*

Papyiform pillars *are pillars designed to look like bundles of papyrus.*

Per ankh *House of Life, the name given to the seat of learning within the temple which educates scribes, priests, and physicians.*

Pylon *large ceremonial gateway to a temple made of two wings with a large doorway in the center. The doors are made of cedar wood inlaid with semi-precious stones.*

Remech *the term the Egyptians use to describe themselves. The term just means "people."*

Sanctuary *the smallest part of the temple, normally at the rear which houses the sacred statue of the god.*

Stela *stone slab with a curved top that is carved with religious imagery or inscriptions.*

Tawy *the term used for Upper and Lower Egypt when they are under control of one ruler. The king would then be referred to as Neb Tawy (Lord of the Two Lands).*

Temple of Millions of Years *the mortuary temple used to worship the ka of a deceased king, maintaining his spirit in the afterlife.*

Tjaty *the vizier, the second in command to the king. The vizier oversees the work in all the palace workshops, construction sites and all the goings on in the palace.*

Upper Egypt *the south of Egypt defined as starting at Mennefer and continuing until the boundaries of Egypt and Nubia.*

Moo *water*

Henqet *beer*

Eerip *wine*

Renpoot *vegetables*

Tee *bread*

Aped-oo *fowl*

Ka-oo *oxen*

Daboo *fig*

Shespet *cucumber*

He *husband*

Humet *wife*

Moot *mother*

It *father*

Kemet *Egypt*

USEFUL PHRASES

Im-eoo em renek?
What is your name?

Renee…
My name is…

Itee pen/Mootee ten/Senee pen
This is my father/mother/brother

Im-eoo chen … Ees/Hoot Netcher/per?
Where is the … tomb/temple/house?

Im-eooish-set eebek m wa/senoo/khemet?
How much for one/two/three?

Im-eoo eebee … Tee/Henket
I would like … bread/beer

Im-eoo earek jar-too-ee er…
Can you ferry me to…

Nefer-wee per pen
This house is beautiful

Im-eoo chen shem-en?
When do we leave?

Reddi hekenoo air-ek.
I give thanks to you (thank you)

Ankh, Oo-jar, Seneb
Life, prosperity, and health

NOTES FOR THE MODERN READER

THE MODERN READER NEEDS TO KNOW THAT THE GUIDE IS INTENDED FOR VISITORS TO THE NATION OF EGYPT, IN PARTICULAR THE CITY OF THEBES, IN THE LATE REIGN OF RAMSES II—USUALLY DATED AROUND 1200 BCE. THE PRESENT TENSE IS USED THROUGHOUT, EXCEPT WHERE THE PAST TENSE IS USED TO SIGNIFY EVENTS EARLIER THAN THE "PRESENT." HERE THE MODERN READER WILL FIND A BRIEF HISTORY TO THE PERIOD FROM THE REIGN OF RAMSES II TO THE ROMANIZATION OF EGYPT. THERE ARE ALSO BRIEF NOTES ABOUT THE SYSTEM OF DATES THAT IS USED, AS WELL AS THE SYSTEM OF MEASUREMENTS.

The reign of Ramses II was a rich one in the history of Egypt—economically, artistically, and architecturally. This book is set in year 65 of Ramses' 67-year reign, at a time all when his achievements were in a state of completion, from the temples of Abu Simbel to his tomb and those of his wife and children.

The reign of Ramses II was the height of the New Kingdom, and after the Kadesh problems in year 5 it was a relatively peaceful time. However, the kings who ruled after Ramses were not to be so lucky.

Ramses was succeeded to the throne by his 13th son, Merenptah, whose short reign was plagued by invasion from the Libyan tribes of the western desert. This Libyan problem only escalated in the reign of Ramses III, who fought a great battle against them in year 5 of his reign, and then against the "Sea Peoples" (who were a conglomerate of numerous foreign tribes) in year 8 of his reign. Although it was a bloody fight, Ramses III proved he was a much better general than Ramses II, and he even directed and won the first naval battle in Egypt's history.

EGYPT DIVIDED

Ramses III is considered to be the last great king of Egyptian history, as after his death Egypt went into a political decline due to numerous divisions within the country, with invading factions ruling from these different centers.

Egypt from the time of Narmer on had always been stronger when united, so this division inevitably caused problems, weakening the power of the throne to such an extent that the High Priests of

Amun were able to take over the Theban area in the 21st Dynasty, even while the king, Ramses XI, was still on the throne. At the same time a group of Libyans gained power in the Delta, followed by Nubians taking control from the high priests, another Libyan dynasty, and then Persians gaining control in the north. Between the 21st Dynasty and the time of Alexander in 332 BCE (a period of about 700 years), the turnover of rulers and dynasties was frequent and somewhat confusing.

After Alexander the Great invaded Egypt, although he maintained the Egyptian religion

MEASUREMENTS

In this book measurements have been given in two forms—the cubit and the deben—whereas the Egyptians actually used a greater range of units.

The *deben* was a measurement of copper or silver, and was used as a standardization for market value, worth approximately 93 g (3.2 oz); obviously silver was more valuable than copper. For smaller amounts there was the *kite*, weighing in at 9–10 g (0.3 oz).

The standardization of liquid measurement was the *hin*, often used for oil and equivalent to roughly 0.47 liters (0.12 gallons).

Grain was measured by the *khar*, which was approximately 75 liters (20 gallons).

Distance was measured in a number of units, although the cubit is the best-known and easiest to envision at approximately 53 cm (21 in) or the distance from the elbow to the fingertips, or the distance between the hands when held shoulder-width apart.

For smaller measurements, hands and fingers were used as measures, with four fingers being the same as one hand. There were seven hands to a cubit.

For larger areas the use of cubits, hands, or fingers was inappropriate, and long distances were therefore measured in *meh-ta* (100 cubits), and large areas in *setjat* or *aurora* (100 square cubits).

and culture, the influx of Hellenes slowly infiltrated the Egyptian culture until it became a hybrid of Egyptian and Greek.

On Alexander's death the throne was inherited by his general Ptolemy I, and thus commenced the Ptolemaic period—a period of 300 years of kings called Ptolemy and queens called Cleopatra, Berenice, or Arsinoe.

The royal turnover was still rapid, and this period saw a decline in Egyptian culture as none of the royal family except the last Cleopatra could even speak Egyptian—isolating the people from their rulers.

THE LOSS OF INDEPENDENCE

The end of Egypt's independent rule came at the death of Cleopatra VII. A period of increasing Roman interference in Egyptian affairs culminated in Octavian (who was later to become the emperor Augustus) invading Egypt and annexing it, making it a province of the Roman Empire.

The Egyptian religion slowly became Romanized, although it was not until the reign of Theodosius in the 4th century CE that the last Egyptian temple was closed and the ability to read hieroglyphs was finally lost.

EGYPTIAN DATES

The ancient Egyptians' calendar was unique and can be confusing. Although their calendar marked off the days of the year, there was no single starting point from which each subsequent year was dated. Instead, at the start of each king's reign the calendar was reset back to year one—hence the passing of time was marked according to the regnal year of the king; for example, year 62 of Ramses II.

It is only when trying to tie these regnal years in with a modern calendar that difficulties occur as we can only base the length of a king's reign on the surviving archeological evidence, as the date of death was never recorded. However, the latest known date of a king is not necessarily the last year of his reign—if something is found with "year 32" of a particular king, it is impossible to know until an artefact is found as proof, that he did not rule for 33, 40, or even 50 years.

Because of this problem our understanding of ancient Egyptian dates is ever-changing and historians often disagree. It is therefore sometimes better simply to refer to regnal dates or dynasties rather than dates BCE.

REFERENCES

The enduring popularity of ancient Egypt means that there are a great many sources to choose from. Alongside the many museums that house Egyptian antiquities around the world, and the countless television documentaries, are a wealth of books and websites.

BOOKS

There are thousands of books on ancient Egypt. Here are a few that are certainly worth reading:

Booth, C., *Ancient Egyptians for Dummies*. If you want a general introduction to all things Egyptian, this is a good place to start. It outlines all aspects of the life and culture of the ancient Egyptians in a fun and easy manner.

Clayton, P., *Chronicle of the Pharaohs* is a more detailed book focusing on all the kings of Egypt. The life, burial, and rule of each king is discussed in as much detail as the archeological evidence allows and this is a good introduction to the rulers of Egypt.

Kitchen, K., *Pharaoh Triumphant* is an invaluable and detailed biography of Ramses II, an enigmatic and fascinating king.

Tyldesley, J., *Ramses: Egypt's Greatest Pharaoh* is a good read for those interested in Ramses II, in whose lifetime this book is set.

WEBSITES

Whilst there are thousands of books on ancient Egypt there are simply countless websites, some of which are better than others.

There are numerous sites that deal with Egyptology as a whole, and one of the best introductory sites is www.touregypt.net, which has articles on virtually every aspect of ancient and modern Egypt and is a good starting point for all research.

If you are looking for more detailed information on historic sites in Egypt then you will find that www.egyptsites.co.uk is a great resource with well-researched information on well-known and obscure sites alike.

There are a number of excavation sites, run by the staff of the projects themselves, which give detailed information on the excavations in progress. The Theban Mapping Project at www.KV5.com is one of the best, providing a detailed record of surveys of the Valley of the Kings, including detailed images of the tomb of Ramses II's sons, KV5, and the great king himself.

INDEX